COACHING
For An Extraordinary Life

BY TERRI LEVINE

COACHING

For An Extraordinary Life

BY TERRI LEVINE

One of America's top

professional coaches shares

techniques you can use

in your everyday life

Ц P

Lahaska Publishing
Buckingham, Pennsylvania

Coaching for an Extraordinary Life

ISBN: 0-9650534-7-4
Library of Congress Control Number: 2001095182

Printed in the United States of America.

Lahaska Publishing
Post Office Box 1147
Buckingham, PA 18912
www. lahaskapublishing.com

Table of Contents

Acknowledgements

This book is dedicated in loving memory to my Mom, Helen Levine, who always supported me, mentored and "coached me" to live my dreams.

And to my extraordinary husband and partner, Mark, who continues to be my supporter, mentor, and my coach and believes in me unconditionally. I am truly blessed by my coaches.

Donna Eliassen for her editing.

Kimberly D'Angelo for her creative designs.

Jim Donovan, my publisher and book coach, for walking beside me throughout this process.

My clients who enrich my life, teach me many lessons, and bring me great joy.

The students at Comprehensive Coaching U for reminding me that everyone benefits from coach training and deserves to learn these tools.

Introduction

The idea for this book came from my work as a professional and personal coach. As I coached people of all ages, all backgrounds, and from all continents, I began to realize the powerful coaching tools I had been using were changing people's lives, as they learned to use these same tools for themselves. Later, through the coach training company that I founded, I learned that many of our students weren't in the training program to be personal and professional coaches, they were there to use the tools to be more effective in their personal and professional lives.

I began to imagine a world where each of us learned these coaching tools, these life tools, as we developed from childhood. I know we'd all be better children, friends, teachers, parents, community members, partners, lovers, business owners, employees ... better people. Coaching tools are really people tools, and I think they need to be made available to the public rather than hidden in coach training programs. We all deserve to have the same skills that coaches have.

I know, from personal experience, that coaches have more evolved lives and are typically happier with who they are and what they do. I know that many people who hire a coach gain this satisfaction with themselves as a benefit of the coaching experience. I began to ask myself, why not give these same coaching tools and gifts to readers who aren't trained as coaches and who may not yet have had a journey with a coach? Why not make these powerful tools available to all to use?

This book is my gift - to share coaching with the world. My desire is that we begin to share these skills with children from an early age, and for us, well, it is never too late to learn!

Happy Coaching!
Terri Levine

Let's Get Oriented

You are now embarking on a wonderful life journey that will change what you do in many ways and allow you to see who you really are inside. This may be scary sometimes and thrilling at others. One thing is for sure, you will know much more about yourself and will have discovered a way to live and work which is beyond your present capacity.

What is necessary for you to begin this journey is that you decide to do the work that goes along with reading this book. This book is simply your guide. You must be accountable and responsible for making the book come alive by doing all the exercises and fully engaging in the process. As in the coaching relationship, the client must do the work to learn and grow.

In our coach training program, we make it clear to new students that they need to do the *practice activities*, engage in the *role plays*, and begin to *work with clients* right away, so that they can begin to do live coaching. This too, is your role as the reader.

Take your time in processing the information. This is not a book to be read quickly or once over. This is a book to be digested, acted upon, re-read, and thought about. It is a fun and delightful process that will enable you to grow.

1

You may feel some of the things don't fit for you or are very difficult for you. That is okay. It is perfectly fine to struggle with new concepts. This is a process, and I am looking for you to feel the growing pains knowing that from this you will progress, even when it feels like you may be standing still.

Imagine me, as your coach for this program, standing by your side, encouraging you and holding you accountable. You bought the book, so you are attracted to self-growth, yes? Now, I am not going to sit here, as your coach, and tell you it is okay not to finish the book or do all the exercises. So imagine you just paid me what a typical coaching client pays for one month of my services, $500 – $1,000 - you don't want to waste this valuable money and not do the work, right? Okay, you are now my coaching client. Get ready, and understand you must make the commitment to do the work and the payoff will be great!

As you embark on this journey, I am by your side as your success partner. Let's get started!

1

An Overview of Basic Coaching Skills

Coaching Skill: Connection

As human beings, we are all connected in some way. Sometimes, we may not see this or may wish we weren't connected to others; however, we are all made of the same stuff and share our humanness. It is essential that we recognize and accept this as our first premise.

WE ARE ALL CONNECTED

The first skill you will begin with as a coach is in recognizing this connection and helping others feel connected to you, while you begin to feel more deeply connected to them. This includes your family, friends, employers, employees, associates, neighbors, community members, etc.—everyone, regardless of your feelings about them.

As a coach, I recognize this sense of connection with everyone in the universe. I recognize that while we are connected, we are each unique and have special gifts, talents, and offerings. This is the wonder of our world and something I appreciate daily.

3

Coaching Skill: Hearing With No Judgment

Understanding that judgment is present in our experiences with other human beings, the first place to work on removing judgment is in our own hearing. As human beings, we tend to put labels on what we hear, such as right or wrong, good or bad, happy or sad, etc. If we shift to a coaching mode, we believe that no one is right or wrong, good or bad … they just *are* and we accept who or what they are, period. Not an easy task, I assure you.

Even young children already hold judgment about what they see and hear and experience and they blurt out their judgment quickly. As you move into the mode of behaving like a coach, remember you are not a young child who goes to the place of criticism, instead, you hold a neutral place with no judgment. After all, who are *you* to be the judge?

Letting go of having a reaction to what others say or do or who they are is very tough. This takes much practice; however, it is a skill worth developing. You can't be connected to others if you aren't willing to accept who or what they are without measurement or reaction.

No ONE IS RIGHT OR WRONG — THEY JUST ARE

Often, new coaches have difficulty practicing non-judgment of people. Somehow, our society has trained us to judge others as good or bad and not to accept those who are different from us or what we consider the "norm." So, this skill takes some work.

To better understand this principle, let's listen in on a typical client session:

Client: *I want to tell you something before we start working together.*

Coach: *Yes, Fred.*

Client: *I just thought you might want to know that I am seriously obese. I don't know if that affects how we work together or not.*

Coach: Not at all.

Client: Because I'm okay with this; it's not something I want to change.

Coach: Okay, and I thank you for putting that out there for me. Whether you're 60 pounds, or 200 pounds, or 6000 pounds, you're still Fred, and I'm excited to work with you.

Client: While we're working together, if I really don't want to do something, maybe I don't want to change my job, how do you deal with that?

Coach: It's really up to you what your goals are. As the Coach, I stand for you as a human being; as a person, I stand for your rights and who you are as an individual, and not for what the goals are that you accomplish. So it's not about what you do or what you accomplish, it's about becoming more you.

Let's listen in on another client session to further understand this principle:

Coach: Tell me more about how you create income so I can better understand.

Client: I'm a professional gambler.

Coach: Okay.

Client: Now, I don't know if that bothers you or not, and I don't want to change that. It's very lucrative.

Coach: Okay, whatever it is that you do is whatever it is that you do to create income. I stand for who you are. So, what is the intent of your coaching with me, Tom?

Client: I just want to be better balanced and be happier. I really don't want to give up my gambling.

Coach: Okay. Does gambling get in the way of your happiness or your balance?

Client: Maybe, sometimes.

Coach: Would you be willing to talk about how that gets in there? I have no judgment, no opinion; it's totally *up to you what you want to do, and it will be throughout all of our coaching.*

Client: *Okay.*

Coach: *Would you allow me to ask you some questions as we do our coaching together, so that you can get honest answers and go deep within yourself to make your own decisions, and just allow me to probe a little deeper than most people have probably probed with you?*

Client: *I think so.*

Coach: *If you're willing, our coaching will work. I do want you to know, if I ever get to a place where it feels uncomfortable, you simply say, "Don't want to go there. Don't want to answer that." Okay?*

Client: *Okay.*

Coach: *Great, and again, Tom, I stand for you; anything and everything you tell me is confidential. It's between us and I hold no judgment.*

Client: *Okay.*

Coach: *Great.*

Let's listen in on still another session:

Coach: *Hi, Sasha!*

Client: *Hi. Are you able to understand me? I have a very heavy accent and I really think that's going to be a problem on the telephone. People have trouble understanding me. Even though I'm really smart, they treat me like I'm dumb because of my accent.*

Coach: *Okay. Are you asking if I have a problem understanding you?*

Client: *Well, yes. Do you have a problem that I'm from the Ukraine, with this heavy accent? You may not want to work with me because of this.*

Coach: *I'm delighted to work with you, and if there is something that I have trouble understanding or you have trouble understanding, let's just honor each other and be sure we ask the other person, or let the other person know that we need some clarification. How's that?*

Client: *Okay.*

Coach: *Great, I'm delighted to work with you.*

Playwork: Whom Do You Judge? How Do You Judge?

Answer the following questions with complete honesty. Put down the first answers that come to you. Answer quickly from your gut, not by listening to your head. Be truthful. This is our starting point, and as your coach, I am trusting you will share everything.

1. List all the names of people you now judge – all of them. Be honest.
2. List the descriptors you use for each person. All of it – even the "nasty" terms that go through your head.

You will later learn tools to take away judgment. Let's imagine this together. What if everyone received this training and no one in the universe judged others? What would/could this world be like? You can create that world for you through your desire to let judgment go. Don't worry, we have many tools to teach you and have only just begun to visit this topic.

Playwork: Hear Without Judgment

Practice listening in a new way - without judgment and from a neutral position, not for who is right or wrong or how you feel about what is said or who is saying it. Practice this exercise right away.

1. Pick three people you will listen to that you already know.
2. Pick two people you will listen to that you haven't yet engaged in a conversation.
3. One of the people on your list needs to come from your earlier exercise—someone you hold in judgment.
4. Before you listen, tell yourself not to think with judgment.
5. Focus on the person you are listening to and not your feelings or what you want to say.
6. Set aside your personal feelings, beliefs, or agendas.
7. Listen to everything as if it was a plain and simple fact and nothing more.
8. Whenever you feel yourself getting emotionally charged or reactive, remind yourself to be quiet and listen.

You will continue to practice this skill as we build up your coaching muscle. When you come from a place of being non-judgmental, you will find you make greater connections with people and that they enjoy being in your presence more. You will also find that as you put judgment aside, you will experience less stress and discomfort. You will spend less time and energy with negative thoughts and more just *being* and letting others *be*.

RECAP: WHAT DID YOU NOTICE?

Coaching Skill: Reflecting Back

When we listen deeply to really get a connection with other human beings, we are able to let them know we have fully understood what they have said by using the skill known as *reflecting back*. This allows the speakers to know that we have really heard them and to correct what we might not have fully understood in their message. This isn't parroting back word for word what is heard. It is a much higher-level skill.

If you have really listened deeply, without judgment, in a way that connects you to another human being, you will hear more than the words the person is saying. You will hear what is underneath those words – what is not spoken. Reflecting back is the way the listener checks in with the speaker to be sure he is heard and understood fully.

Let's listen in on another client session to further understand this principle:

Coach: *Hello Jim, what's up for you today?*

Client: *Well, you know, I've really been getting overwhelmed here. I have so much stuff going on, doing a lot of different things, and I'm running five or six projects, and I seem to be going in circles, and I just don't know what's happening. Everyone seems to be not taking care of what they should be doing and are out to get me… just going nuts here.*

Coach: *So, what I'm hearing is that you're in a place of feeling some real overwhelm; you're feeling a little bit out of control, and there is a lot going on with other people beyond your circumstances, is that right?*

Client: *Yes, I just feel that I have no control over what they are doing, and it's affecting me, and I don't know what to do about it.*

Coach: *Okay. So, you're also feeling the lack of control and then it sounds like it raises the question, "What do I do with all of this?"*

Client: *Yes, I guess that's really the question. What do I do?*

Coach: *So, what I'm hearing, Jim, just try this on and see what you think… it sounds like you're very concerned and very focused right now on all the stuff that's coming up and what's going wrong.*

Client: *Yes, everything seems to be going wrong at the moment and I don't know what to do.*

Coach: *Okay. So, the overall thing that I would like to speak about for a few minutes is what I heard, which is things are going wrong, they're all out of control. Yes?*

Client: *Yes!*

Coach: *Okay, great.*

Playwork: Reflect Back

Connect with speakers by letting them know you get the emotion and feelings as well as the words and the verbal message. Practice this right away. Try it with a person you are close to, someone you don't know as well, and someone who was on your original judgment list in the first exercise.

1. Listen without reaction or judgment.
2. Listen to the words.
3. Listen to the emotion, the tone, and the concepts.
4. Check in with the speaker by telling them what you believe you heard them say and ask them if you were right. You can express this with phrases like, "What I think you are saying is …" or "Is this correct…?" or "Did I hear you say…?" or "Is this what you meant by…?"
5. Do not come from a place of assessing or agreeing or disagreeing with the speaker. Come from a sense of pure, non-judgmental, and fully connected listening.

This is a coaching skill that has an amazing effect on those we communicate with. Most people want more than anything to be heard - really, deeply, fully heard. It is rare that anyone really listens to us in this way. I can think of many times when speaking with bosses, where they were busy shuffling papers on their desks, or taking phone calls, or reading e-mail. I can think of times when family members were more engaged in TV than in listening to me. And I am guilty of being distracted by my own thoughts and also of judging what the other person was saying. If you master this skill, and I believe you can and will if you really choose to, you will have greatly impacted the lives of others. Children have a great desire for people to understand them (don't we all?) and they so appreciate when someone takes the time and energy to really care about what they have to say. Become an expert at reflecting back. The payoff is high!

RECAP: WHAT DID YOU NOTICE?

Coaching Skill: Responding

Okay, now you have fully heard other people and are listening from a place of being connected and letting go of all judgment. You are well on your way to better understanding the basic coaching skills. You are reflecting back, so both you and the speaker are clear that you fully understand his message and his emotions beyond the words. Now it is time for you to let the speaker know that you heard him in a deep way. Your reply will reinforce that you are non-judgmental about what you heard and realize the connection of his humanity to yours and that you accept and appreciate who he is.

We have a pattern of response where while the speaker is talking, we are already thinking about what we want to say next, or what we want to say in response to what we heard, or what our ego thinks about what has been said. It is time to break that pattern because we can't listen deeply when we are formulating responses. It is time to respond after we have reflected back and are clear we heard the speaker's message fully. Then our response isn't about us, it is to let the speaker know we heard him and he is understood.

Let your instinct, not your ego, be your guide.

Let's listen in again on one of our client sessions:

Coach: *Joan, what's going on?*

Client: *I just had the worst day at work that you could ever imagine. I don't believe the people I have to deal with. The boss I have, this woman, she's just crazy. She's making me crazy and she thinks everybody should drop what they are doing and just run around and respond to her. She's just totally out of control, disorganized, and I don't know what to do. I can't afford to quit. I don't know! I just don't know what to do.*

Coach: *Okay, so what I absolutely hear here is a lot of frustration, yes?*

Client: *Oh yeah! I can't quit; I can't afford to quit. I don't know if I can get another job somewhere, I don't know if I can work with this woman; she's crazy; she just thinks everybody in the world revolves around her and I should just give up my life and drop things because she needs them done at the last minute. I don't know what my options are or where I can go with this.*

Coach: *You sound like you have a lot of anger, and are you also feeling stuck, like there is nothing you can do; you're helpless in this situation?*

Client: *Yeah, I feel like I should either quit or cave into her demands. I don't know if there are any other options.*

Coach: *Okay, before we start looking at options, I just want to be really clear that I am understanding what you're feeling. It is the anger, the frustrations, and feeling kind of like they are not in your control because you're feeling stuck?*

Client: *Yes, exactly.*

Coach: *Okay, great.*

Client: *You know, Terri, the real problem here is that I can't talk to anybody. I talk to my friends and I talk to my family, and I talk to my husband; they all think that because I have this big paying job that I should just put up with it and just hang in there and not mind it because they are paying me a lot of money to put up with this kind of stuff and it goes with the territory. I'm just going in circles and I'm frustrated and angry. Nobody understands it. I'm the only one that can relate to this.*

Coach: *Well, let me just say that you're not alone; I'm here with you and I do relate to it. I really am with you and want for you to move through this, and I really see you moving into something that feels rewarding and fun and joyful, and so you do have a partner in this, Joan.*

Client: *That's nice to hear, because you see, you're the only one that understands.*

Coach: *Sometimes one cheerleader is enough, yes?*

Client: *Yeah, that's true, I guess.*

Coach: *Great, and I'm delighted to be your cheerleader, so let's take a look together at some possibilities, because I think there are some.*

Client: *Okay.*

Let's listen in again on one of our client sessions:

Client: *As I said before, I'm really overweight but I would really like to just leave that alone. I don't really think that's really an issue. That's not what is making me unhappy. I'm perfectly happy being overweight.*

Coach: *I've noticed that you've brought this topic up a couple of times, and so I would like to ask you what it is about the weight that you're happy with.*

Client: *I don't want to change.*

Coach: *And I would also like to ask you what it is about the weight that makes you go immediately to a posturing of "I don't want to change it."*

Client: *Other people seem to think I should want to change, because they're thin, and I should want to be thin, and I should want to be like them. I tried that and that was really hard, and I just can't do that*

13

*anymore. So I'm not. And I've accepted the way
that I am and that's that.*

Coach: *Okay, so is it about the weight being just too hard
to deal with? There is something here underneath,
about the too hard to deal with that keeps surfacing,
so what is your real truth here?*

Let's listen in again on another of our client sessions:

Client: *As I said before, I'm just angry, frustrated, and fed-
up, and I don't know what to do about this, and I
just go in circles, and I can't quit, and I can't
change, and I can't stay, and I guess I'm just stuck
and there is nothing I can do about it.*

Coach: *It sounds like you're in a place of really looking at
everything that's wrong. Can you shift with me?
Can you now tell me everything that is right in
this situation?*

Client: *Right? I don't know if there is anything right. This
woman is crazy that I happen to work for; I guess
the right is. . .*

Coach: *Let me interrupt. Just tell me one right thing,
without anything wrong. Okay?*

Client: *I get paid really well.*

Coach: *Great! So you get paid really well. What else is
working; what else is right here?*

Client: *I like what I do.*

Coach: *That's great! What else is working?*

Client: *I like the business, the company, and the industry.*

Coach: *Great! You like the business, you like the company,
and you like the industry. What else is right?*

Client: *I guess a couple of times I did go out to lunch with
this woman and she was "okay." I guess, maybe if I
could find a way to deal with her...*

Coach: *Okay, let's stop at the lunch part. So, sometimes
she's okay. Right? What else is right?*

Client: *I don't know; now you have me digging.*

Coach: *The thing I want you to take a look at is that you are noticing everything that is wrong, but it's not a problem to do that, because we're human, and we do that. So I'm not saying "Oh, that's bad to do." I'm just saying, "That's really human of you." All I want you to do is shift with me and move to a place of looking at some of the things that are right so we take you out of that state of blame, frustration, and feeling like a victim. And my question to you is, "What can you do to empower yourself?"*

Client: *That's a good question.*

Playwork: Respond From Your Heart

When we have clearly understood a speaker and are ready to respond, the response comes from our hearts and not our heads. Our heads tend to formulate stories about us, or defend our ego, or judge who people are, or what people have said. Our heart, our instinct, allows us to speak to show understanding and connection. The shift here is to get in touch with your instinct and say what is in your heart and not go to your head in formulating a response. I have a strong belief in people, and I know that people have great things to say to acknowledge each other – even without coach training. We haven't done it much, so we fear that we won't know what to say. I know with certainty that if you follow your gut instincts, then you already know how to be a great coach and know what to say that will show you listened and connected with the speaker.

1. Focus on the speaker and listen at a deep level to be connected.
2. Let judgment go.
3. Get out of your head and your ego and let your gut instincts take over.
4. Respond once you have fully understood the message and reflected it back and are clear you heard the speaker.

5. Say what is in your gut that shows you are connected in some way to the speaker and are supportive of them and not judgmental of them.
6. Practice this in five interactions a day, with five different speakers a day, each and every day until it becomes a habit.

There you have the basic coaching tools you will need to be a great coach and live a life that is more fulfilling, a life that will bring more rewarding relationships, greater success, and more enjoyment to you. Now we will get into the meat of how to make these skills work for you and how to enhance these skills to build upon them more fully. We will then add the more advanced coaching tools you will need to create new relationships and a more rewarding life. Buckle your seat belts; we haven't begun to fly yet!

RECAP: WHAT DID YOU NOTICE?

2

Tuning In:
The Art of Deep Listening

There is no coaching skill more important than tuning in. Tuning in is the deepest form of listening. It is the type of listening that we are rarely engaged in as we raise our children, rush to our work, run endless errands, multi-task everything, and are pushed and pulled by an active, out of balance lifestyle and way of being. Tuning in means we give up the focus being about us and turn all of our attention to the speaker. We forget about our own agenda or our own thoughts and fully, with intention, focus on what the speaker is saying, because we want to get a true sense of who they are and where they are coming from. We give up our attachments and our judgments and set aside our own thoughts and stories. We engage deeply and meaningfully in being connected by hearing others.

Although we hear with our ears, we don't often listen with our hearts. Our ears get the words, the language, and then our heads go racing ahead to form our own responses or connections and feed them back to "us." We can't wait to say something about our experiences, how we feel, or what we know. We want the conversation to be focused on our greatness or our needs. You might feel defensive about this statement, and I request for now that you just let it sit with you and let the judgment go. Come from a place of not feeling defensive against what I say that you might not agree with, to a place of just letting it be ... take it as my fact ... listen to it as you will when you tune into the speakers you will be listening to.

Tuning in not only involves hearing, it involves hearing what is not said or is non-verbally conveyed to us, and it involves listening for emotion, tone, and pain. It is about what lies behind the words the speaker utters.

As a coach, you will listen in a new way and be fully tuned in to connect with people. This will be one of the greatest tools that will bring you a closer sense of who you are and who others are and allow for meaningful, deep connections with everyone in your life.

Before you can tune in, you must quiet your own mind. We often have so many things we are thinking about at once that we just can't keep focused on the speaker. With practice and desire, you will be able to get your mind to be still so that you can tune in.

BE INTERESTED NOT INTERESTING

Playwork: Notice

If you listen to the conversations of those around you, you will notice the speakers use the word "I" throughout their conversations. In fact, most of the time, speakers are focused on what it is they want to say, not what the other person is saying. We will begin your tuning in work by discovering how others communicate and by noticing their listening patterns.

1. Listen each day to at least three different speakers engaged in conversations.

2. Try to guess or count how many times in about five minutes of conversation the speakers use the word "I".

3. Try to guess or count how many times the speakers complete a thought or sentence for each other.

4. Try to guess or count how many times the speakers interrupt each other.

5. Listen for how often the speakers make each other wrong or judge each others' comments.

6. In a five-minute conversation with another, do not use the word "I" at all. Ask the other person to keep track of each time you use the word "I".

You may find out some pretty amazing things as you do this exercise. My first time through, I was shocked at the interruptions, and the arguing of points, and how frequently I heard "I". Then I believed I wasn't as guilty of this as others. I taped a five minute conversation and then counted the "I's", the interruptions, and the judgment. I couldn't believe that this was me! I was trained as a Speech-Language Pathologist and fully believed that I had a great listening skill. I found out I had a lot to learn.

In order to tune in, we need to allow ourselves to be completely and fully present for the speaker. Since you are now listening for the meaning behind the words, this is a skill that takes practice and concentration. No longer are you just hearing information. You are actively trying to understand the information and do so without bringing in your agenda, judgment, opinions, or beliefs as the listener. You are going to be fully present and put your own thoughts aside. To do this, you will need to clear your head and make space for the listener. There are many things that get in the way as we listen. To be fully present you will want to shed those things.

One thing that prevents people from tuning in is that they are thinking about themselves, how they are right, or what it is they want to say to the speaker. They are focused on themselves and what they want to communicate. If you are tuned in and are fully present, your ego will not be involved in your listening. You will be fully present to the speaker and her message. You will let your own stuff float away, to be focused. One of the ways that we hinder our tuning in is when we listen and relate what we believe is important, debatable, or when we start defending for or against the message. Many times when listening, people get caught up in their own beliefs, values, and emotions, and how they differ from what the speaker is saying.

If you are tuned in and fully present, you will set all your personal thoughts about the message aside and accept completely, without judgment, what the speaker is saying. No agreement, no disagreement. What she is saying is simply her truth. As a coach, we accept the client and her truth and set our own truth aside to create that listening space.

Part of this is not being attached to the outcome of what the speaker is saying or where the speaker is going. It isn't about listening so that you can then communicate to the speaker what you believe or what you want her to do, think, or feel. There is absolutely no agenda that you hold for the speaker. You are just there to be tuned in – to foster the connection from human being to human being. You don't lead, manipulate, motivate, or sell anyone on anything. You simply tune in.

As you tune in, you put all your own judgments on a shelf. You aren't listening to see if the speakers are good or bad or are right or wrong. You are accepting them and what they have to say. Their values, beliefs, and agenda may be very different from yours. Don't substitute yours for theirs. They have their own make-up. Acknowledge them. Honor the fact that we are all connected yet we are all unique beings. That is the beauty of our humanness. We don't need to look, act, or be alike. We are wonderful exactly as we are. Celebrate differences and notice connections.

LISTEN WITH YOUR HEART

Playwork: Create Listening Space

It is now time for you to practice the art of tuning in by creating a new way to listen. Your listening will be fully about hearing the speaker and will have nothing to do with you. This will be a new experience and will develop your tuning in skill.

1. Go back to the first exercise and pick a person you hold judgment about.
2. Engage them in a conversation.
3. During the conversation, allow the speaker to fully communicate, and listen with your heart.
4. Let ALL judgment go.
5. Don't bring up your attachment, agenda, or beliefs.
6. What is in the way? Identify everything that is coming up for you. Notice what is making tuning in difficult.

The role of the coach is to be with the speaker and be fully engaged in each conversation. To do this, we must begin to accept some coaching premises. If we hold any belief about others needing fixing or being imperfect, then we will go to the place of judgment, of wanting to fix, of knowing better, and having the answers. It is very important for us to hold a vision that each speaker is just perfect as he is. Not our version of perfect (remember, no judgment!) ... just perfect. If we stay with the premise that we are all connected, then we believe we are all made of the same wonderful stuff and each human being is exactly as he is meant to be. We stop trying to change or improve others to meet our standards or to believe what we believe. Is our vision right? Are we more perfect than another? I think not.

If we give up wanting to change others and wanting to give them our beliefs and agenda and convince them to believe what we believe, then we will get the connections of their values, their goals, their beliefs. We will hear their agenda and not lead them to ours. Our own self-serving interests are pushed aside to create the space for them to *be*. We hear where they are, who they are, and we fully accept them. We don't judge, we don't convince, and we never let our own agenda get in the way. Each person on the planet is the way he is and who he is because he is perfectly created to be this way. Sounds challenging, yes? Sure it is. No one said this was easy. To be a great coach, we must work through all the things that don't fit for us right now.

The first time someone told me that a client of mine was "perfect," I had trouble seeing it. The client had been in jail and was doing many things that seemed unethical and immoral to me. Oh yes, I was judging, bringing my beliefs and values to the situation. No doubt about it – guilty again! Then I made the shift to believe that the client was where he was because he was meant to be there today. That was perfect for him today or in this life experience. It didn't mean I couldn't hold a higher vision or energy for the client. It didn't mean I couldn't believe the client would have a more joyful life. I could hold high visions and belief in who the client was. For today, for the lesson he is here to learn, he is perfect, and I accept him without judgment. It takes time to get to this place, so don't worry if you are thinking, "I couldn't shift that fast and believe in this client" ... I thought the same thing. With a desire and with practice, you will be a great coach.

WE ARE PERFECT AS WE ARE

So, there you are accepting the client and letting your judgment go and being fully tuned in. Now you are listening on a deep level. As speakers give us information, we begin to hear their habits and patterns. Sometimes, they may converse about their work or their family or relationships with friends and associates. These are prominent themes in people's lives. Another theme that often shows up in adults has to do with money. This is one I see frequently in my coaching clients, as well. Of course, speakers also let you in on their feelings and ideas about themselves. We just love talking about ourselves.

As you listen, think about what patterns are repeating themselves and how the speakers show us their habits and how these habits might be keeping them stuck where they are. When we hear others are trapped by their patterns, we can later use our coaching tools to help them move beyond what is keeping them back. But first we have to listen deeply to recognize where and why they are stuck.

People are often kept in the same place or mode because they have a habit of using negative energy. Negative energy is like spinning your wheels. You don't move forward and often keep complaining about the same situation over and over again. For a year, I talked about wanting to re-pot my plants. I could give you 15 reasons why I couldn't do it. Meanwhile, my plants kept on growing beyond their pots and I kept talking. I also continued to bring more plants into my home while I wasn't even caring for the older plants. I was stuck. I spent a lot of energy thinking about my plants and talking about them versus taking care of them. This energy could have been spent on caring for them or moving on. I was in a rut.

Another thing that keeps people stuck is their lack of belief in themselves. They beat themselves up for everything they are doing wrong or failing at. One of my good friends, who I adore, has been telling herself she "can't lose weight"… she "can't hold down a job" … she is "no good at sports." She never speaks about her successes (and I see many of them!). If she does something human, like drop her car keys, she reacts by saying something like, "how stupid of me." I hear that she is stuck in a lack of belief about how great she really is.

Many of my coaching clients are stuck because of fear. There are many different types of fears: fear of failure, fear of success, fear of dying, fear of trying, fear of others, fear of self, etc. No matter what the fear, once we help the speakers to identify it, it can be a starting point for them to move past it. So listen for the fears. Notice the fears showing up that are holding people back.

Have you ever listened to people who sounded like the entire world was out to get them? I often hear people speaking about their employers with terms like "they did this and it isn't fair" and talking about people they are in a relationship with as "he/she did this to me." Instead of wearing the martyr hat, we can help people see how they actually have control and choice in their lives. For now, tune in to see if people are wearing the martyr hat.

What about the people who seem to have some deep issues that really need therapy or are in therapy? They need us to listen and deserve our attention just as much as the people who aren't stuck. Typically, a therapy issue means these people just can't move forward. So, listen to them and acknowledge them. They will be thankful to be heard in a new way, too.

I AM HERE TO HEAR YOU

Playwork: Hearing Habits

It is now time to do some of the work. We will begin by helping you see what might be holding you back and then move on to develop your skill of hearing what holds others back. You will begin to know yourself more through this exercise.

1. Tune in to one of your own conversations. What do you hear? What is holding you back? What habits do you have in your life that are keeping you from having what you want in your life? Be honest. Go deep.
2. Tune into one conversation each and every day, and listen for the habit that is holding the other person back. Label it. Identify it.

Just as you can listen for habits that keep people stuck, you can listen for the habits that empower people to leap ahead. These patterns have to do with what people are really, strongly convinced about and believe deeply inside of them - it is a part of who they are. I think the number one pattern that moves people forward is one of their values. What are they firmly committed to, and what principles guide them in living their life?

People have their own guides or inner principles that they operate from. We have our own sense of integrity and of what is right and what is wrong. When we have a goal or a plan, we get most excited and inspired by the ones that match our principles. We easily get pulled toward these habits.

As we move towards the habits that support us and align with our integrity, we feel positive and our energy feels right. We then see our own wins and feel good about ourselves when our values are met. Whenever our self-esteem is high, then we feel like we are on top of the world. We feel good about our capabilities and ourselves and are proud of who we are and of our accomplishments. We hold ourselves in high regard and feel more valuable in our contributions.

Each human being is unique and lives by his or her own set of rules and limits. A rule is a principle or a belief that we follow and that we live by for ourselves and in our behavior. For example, my guiding principle might be that I will not curse.

We also have limits that we use to keep safe from the behaviors of others. These are things we are not willing to tolerate from other people. So, I may also set the limit that I won't allow others to curse in front of me.

These self-imposed rules and limits differ for each of us and allow us to make decisions more quickly and to know what we want and who we choose to be with. Limits help protect us from other people and keep our integrity in our own beliefs, values, and principles.

We also follow habits that allow us to work at our best, or be our best in a natural, easy, effortless way. I refer to this with my clients as being in flow. We flow most when the things we do match our values and are easy to be attracted to.

You will notice that every one of us, while connected as human beings, has very different patterns and habits that move us towards our personal growth and evolution. Imagine if each of us had a better sense of what worked for us. Imagine being able to quickly and easily say yes or no to decisions, people, and choices. Imagine encouraging friends and family and colleagues to provide their own answers and to know their own wishes by matching their values and making choices right for them - not choices that another person values - but that are their own unique values.

I know that as I honor my own values and as I practice habits that support my beliefs, I feel greater self-esteem, greater connection to society, and make a stronger contribution to those in my life. It is easy to be myself because I have stopped coming from a place of wondering who or what was judging me. Do you know what makes you feel happiness? I mean really deep feelings of joy? What is a delight for you? What brings delight to you?

It is interesting that most people have difficulty answering these questions. It is also interesting that sometimes someone outside of us can notice what brings us happiness. So, if we are going to make a difference to others, we can begin by noticing the habits and patterns that create more joy in their lives. We can support their healthy habits and patterns and point them out to others. I love using this tool as a coach to help my clients create extraordinary happiness at work and in their lives.

MY PURPOSE IS TO CREATE JOY
FOR MYSELF AND OTHERS

Playwork: Greatness

As you continue to listen to conversations with others and of your own dialogue, you will want to focus on what makes you feel more positive about yourself and what makes others feel more greatness in them. Perhaps this sounds conceited to you when thinking about greatness in yourself … I say, "*yes*" … if you don't think you are great, then how can you be great at living your life, doing your work, loving your partner or your kids or your church? We are all great … in different, unique, and wonderful ways.

1. Listen as you speak, and begin to think about the things you find joyful about *you*.
2. Listen to people's conversations and be in tune with their values. Notice their self-esteem.
3. Write a list of your most important rules and limits. Where are you not following them?
4. One day this week, find at least one habit that is positive in all the people you speak with. Focus only on their greatness and then share it with them.
5. Keep being in tune with others and focusing on being interested in them, rather than impressing them with how interesting you are.
6. Listen to connect. Listen because you care.

Most of us don't really listen. While the other person is speaking, we are thinking about what we are going to say, or what we have to add, or something about ourselves.

Sometimes we can't even wait for the other people to finish speaking. We want to complete their thoughts; we already know what they are going to say, and we can't wait to add our own two cents. Very often while we're listening, we're so much in touch with what's in our own heads that we are not listening with open ears and with a deep sense of connection and with a caring heart. We are often focused on ourselves, where we are, and where we want to be. This is your opportunity to listen in a great way rather than to be great.

3

Leaping Over
the Critical Gap

As we listen, we will notice that people talk a lot about what they want and what they'd like to achieve - their wishes, their hopes, their dreams, and their plans. If we're really listening, and again, that means being deeply connected with both our heart and our head, then we will understand the discrepancies between where people are today and where they want to go, or what they want to get, or what they see themselves achieving. Let's face it, all of us want things that we don't currently have. All of us talk about things that we don't currently see. We have dreams, we have wishes, we have wants, and we have goals. In coaching, we actually call this a critical gap. The critical gap is the place between where we currently are and where we want to go. It's that void; it's that blank space. There are many ways that people express their critical gaps. As we're listening deeply, we may hear that they don't have enough limits or enough rules in place to help them achieve what they want. I'm sure you can think of people who are in a state of overwhelm; or what about those people who can never say "no" and keep adding more and more to their plate?

In business, I work with a lot of people who lack the ability to manage their time well or to be well organized. What about people who lack their own self-worth and consistently compare themselves to others and put themselves down? As we listen to others, we can hear how they see themselves and how they might not see all their current greatness, or their value, or how they might not believe in achieving their own goals, because they don't think they have the abilities or capabilities. As we listen to others, we will always hear critical gaps and what they are missing in terms of resources or support to move them forward. It could be that they are missing people, it could be that they are missing connections, it could be that they missing external or internal motivators. I listen carefully, as the coach, to learn what's missing in the areas of relationships, love, money, strength, willingness, readiness, and support.

Another gap that comes up a lot in being human, is a gap in real commitment; we talk about dreams, we talk about goals, but we haven't set in motion any plan to achieve them. These are not burning desires in our heart that we absolutely want to achieve. I find a lot of times when people have a gap in making their goals happen, they do have a gap in their commitment, and they have a lot of ideas and a lot of thoughts, but that's all they are. There is no plan; there is no action taken toward achieving them.

Other gaps include gaps in direction. I think I want to go here; I think I want to go there; not being really sure where I want to go. Not having that internal guiding system that comes from having a great burning desire within you. Some of the external gaps that I hear frequently are about money. Let's face it, as human beings that's something we all seem to want and we don't seem to believe we have enough. Even those people I know whom I consider very wealthy like to continue to invest and continue to earn more money. So we may hear people talk about their gaps in money, they want more money, they're losing money, they'd like to hang on to money longer, or their business isn't as profitable as it could be or should be.

There are also gaps in knowledge. I just don't have the right skills; I don't have the right information; if only I had more experience; if only I had better training. So again, it's where people currently are versus where they see themselves in the future.

One other gap I want to mention is the gap in professional assets. The gap could be having professional people or a network to help you, support you, and guide you; it could be knowing the right people in a certain industry; and it could be having the right support, resources, or advice. So when you're wearing your coaching hat, tune in to the blocks that people have in moving forward, the blocks that people have in achieving their goals. We can actually help other people move forward and achieve what they talk about wanting to become their reality.

Playwork – The Critical Gap

1. Listen to people talk and focus on hearing their critical gap.
2. Note your own critical gaps. What is it you are wanting in your life, business, family, from your children, etc. that you don't yet have? What is the gap?

When you listen for and identify the critical gap in both yourself and in other people, notice how it becomes clear and obvious how much we are wanting, and what is holding us back. By becoming a coach of your own mind and by coaching those who surround you and who you come into contact with, you will discover that you have this great untapped ability to move people forward and that you will achieve things beyond your greatest dreams in an effortless way. It is also a wonderful experience to be able to see what is holding other people back, to help them identify where their critical gap may be, and then coach them to leap over that gap and on to the next plane.

USING QUESTIONS THAT ARE POWERFUL

Most human beings communicate by using statements and questions. In fact, if you think about it, much of our life is spent asking ourselves questions, either verbally or non-verbally. For example, this morning when I woke up, I had to decide what I was going to wear, what kind of soap I was going to use on my face, what I wanted to eat for breakfast, which shoes looked right with my outfit, and if I needed to bring a coat or a jacket based upon the weather, etc. We are constantly making these decisions by asking ourselves questions. Sometimes we ask the questions verbally, and often we just go through this process of questioning and making choices without even realizing it. In coaching, we use questions to help people uncover their own truths. These truths are something that many of us don't recognize, because we do so many things in our life experience that are about pleasing others, doing what is right, doing what's wrong, doing what we're told we "should" do, so that very often, we don't even know what our own honest behaviors and thought patterns are, or even who we are.

As coaches, we have the wonderful tool of using questions in a powerful way to help find answers and discover in a crystal clear way what is true about our own being and our own essence. Questions can help people become very focused on what actions to take. There is a difference between asking a question versus asking what we call "powerful questions." Very often, we ask questions that are not very important, nor do they create a powerful answer. For example, when I pass someone on the street who I know as an acquaintance and say, "How are you today?", typically I'm not really listening, nor am I interested in her response. I'm hoping to hear, "I'm fine. How are you?" and then just move about my business. The question is not powerful; the question here aims simply to gather data, gather some information, or is a social pleasantry. The distinction in asking a powerful question is that a powerful question is actually not used just to get information; it is used to help people become clearer about their purpose, or their actions, or who they are, and also to help them move forward and move through that critical gap more swiftly. Powerful questions are an amazing tool that we can use for ourselves, as well as to help children, parents, friends, family, and colleagues make very large gains in their lives.

In order to move people forward by asking powerful questions, you must first tune in, remembering that tuning in is the way to be fully present, fully hearing, and fully listening to people. It is important to remember that this is always the first critical tool in the coaching process. So first you listen to get in tune with where the other people are, and what it is that they want, or they need, or they would like to have. As we become more tuned in, it becomes easier to see where other people are at and what's important to them. Then, we will also know which powerful questions to ask that will move them forward. While we are in tune, we also want to comprehend at a deep level both what the other people say and what they don't say. When you comprehend very deeply, it is easier to know the right questions to ask. Another part about asking the powerful question is also being very prepared for the response that may come. I find that powerful questions tend to generate pretty powerful responses; doesn't that make sense? Some of the powerful questions that I ask can cause some emotion, or they can cause some action, or they can cause people to stop and enter into a deep and meaningful thought process. I know that I've asked a powerful question of my clients when there is either a reaction, or they tell me, "Gee Terri, that's a great question," or they simply stop and become quiet. No matter what the response is, I'm always prepared and will always be there to support my clients, whatever their reactions, in a non-judgmental way.

So let's understand what a powerful question is. A powerful question is a question that is based upon what you have heard the other person say, what you have heard he or she really wants, and what the blockages are. It's a way of saying, "How can I help this person leap through the critical gap?" It's asking yourself, "What's the most important thing I could ask this person right now that will allow her to see new possibilities, or allow her to create new behaviors, or to get into motion right now. A powerful question is about where the other person is today, right now, in the present, and where they want to go in the future.

When I ask a powerful question of either myself or of my clients, many times it has resulted in simply stopping a habitual pattern. It encourages my client to be silent and to do some reflecting, and then to be very conscious and present in making his or her own decisions. And knowing that no matter what a client says to me, I will be here in a non-judgmental way to hear and to listen to her. Powerful questions also help me get to my own truth very quickly. What is it that I really want? What is it that will allow me to experience my life in the way that I choose?

So, to prepare yourself for powerful questions, you must be ready for whatever answer comes up, and you need to listen and be fully present in a way that supports the other person without holding any judgment.

As you may have guessed, sometimes it is very difficult to ask powerful questions. Powerful questions can evoke a lot of emotion and may be uncomfortable for you to ask or for the other person to hear. Whenever I have a question that either comes into my head, as kind of a gut reaction, or I get an inkling that perhaps I should say it, I allow myself to just go ahead and ask the uncomfortable question. That is usually the powerful question; it's the one that needs to be asked and the one that needs to be asked the most.

When I formulate a powerful question, I do it in a very simple way so that I'm asking it in a manner that the other person can hear and understand easily and using the same language they have used in speaking with me. I only ask one powerful question at a time, and I keep the question focused primarily on the one issue or the one item where I identified the critical gap, and which, I believe, will move the other person forward.

So what happens after I ask the question? Quite simply, I just sit and close my mouth. May sound easy, but it's not. Sometimes powerful questions will result in the other person just becoming silent. Sometimes it will result in the other person becoming offended. Sometimes it will result in the other person becoming defensive. It will always have a result. You know a powerful question has landed on its target, because typically, there will be some energy and attention and focus given to the answer by the person you are speaking with. Being an experienced coach, I know when I've asked a powerful question because the client suddenly stops, or comments on the question itself, or simply shifts his or her energy and starts talking about something else.

Let's listen in on another client session to further understand this principle:

Client: *Terri, I've spent all this money and time to go to medical school and I come out and here I am, me and my stethoscope; I have my office, everything is set-up and between the HMO's and everything that is going on in healthcare today, I'm having the hardest time building a practice. They don't teach us about the business in medical school. They teach you how to be a great doctor, and I am a great doctor. I just don't know how to get patients, what do I do? I don't know if I can make it.*

Coach: *Is there a real drive, or motivation to be a business owner?*

Client: *That is a great question. I need to think... Well, I went into medicine because I wanted to be a great doctor.*

Coach: *That's why I'm asking you if it's about being a business owner...*

Client: *I want to be a country doctor. I want my own practice and I want my own patients and I want to be able to take care of people.*

Coach: *Could you be a country doctor, and a great country doctor, taking care of people without having your own business?*

Client: *I guess, I could join someone else's practice. That might be a possibility, but I don't want to be involved with these big factory kind of practices, where they just pass people through the office. I want to give people attention; I want to really take care of them. That's why I do this.*

Coach: *What I'm seeing here is that your focus is around the patients, and it's not necessarily about being a business owner. In our work together, I've noticed the subject of owning a business seems to be the idea that you don't enjoy. Do you really want to run your own business?*

Client: *I'm a doctor. Not a business owner. It's something I have to do if I want to have my own practice. I have to find some way to get the patients. How else can I get patients to come in here?*

Coach: *My observation here is that you're a doctor, you're a great doctor, and really at the heart of the matter is that's what you want to be.*

Client: *Yes.*

Let's listen in again on another session:

Coach: *I'm going to ask you to notice and observe with me that you've gone to the place of looking at being a higher and better person than she is. I'd like for you to hold the idea that she's not right, she's not wrong, she just "is" and love her as she is. And let's look at some of the things that are making you uncomfortable. Only you can deal with you and your feelings, and what I was observing is that you were trying to have her be the one who changes. It just doesn't work that way in the universe. We can only control one person and that's "us". Would you be willing to look at that with me?*

Client: *I guess I could look at that, yes.*

Coach: *Why do you feel you are better than she is? What is your evidence?*

Client: *I don't want to come off that way. I guess I have been, huh?*

THE POWER OF POWERFUL QUESTIONS

Playwork

1. Today as you listen deeply, ask each person that you are in conversation with a minimum of one powerful question.
2. Ask yourself at least one powerful question today that will move you forward through something that you are dealing with.
3. As you go through your day, listen to see if anyone asks you a powerful question that stops you, creates new thoughts for you, or moves you forward.

Powerful Observations

We've already talked about powerful questions, and powerful observations share many of the same characteristics. Of course, the basics for making observations has to do with tuning in to other people and really being able to hear them deeply, being ready for whatever response they come up with, and I will also add, being ready to be completely honest.

Very often in our society we are taught to tell little white lies, or to be polite, or not to tell the whole story, or simply to hide our own truth. But if we are all behaving as human beings who are now practicing a coaching philosophy, then we'll all be united in wanting to be honest and truthful with one another. Simply put, a powerful observation is about what we have perceived as the listener and what we believe is the truth. It doesn't mean that the listener will accept the truth, or believe the truth, or agree with our truth. It simply is our truth, and it's a truth that we have been taught to withhold. So, one of the coaching tools that you will now be using is being ready and comfortable in saying what it is you hear, even if that does cause a bit of a reaction in the speaker.

What is different about powerful observations versus our everyday observations is that one is thought provoking while the other is often mundane in nature. We go through life making many observations each moment. "I don't like the pants you're wearing." "You're in a bad mood today." "Let me tell you how you did that wrong." "Let me tell you how to do it right." We continually make observations, and very often, these are quiet, in our head conversations. A powerful observation has a purpose, a coaching purpose. It's a way of getting the speaker to stop and really take a look at what it is she is saying, and certainly, it's a way to move her through the critical gap. Powerful observations must always be truthful. It's about what has come up for us based on what we've heard the other person say. It's our belief and we're willing to speak it completely. It's important here not to want to go to a place of making the other person wrong or making ourselves right. A powerful observation is simply a way of saying this is what I think, this is my opinion, and it is not an absolute truth, it's just the truth that I hear in this particular moment. The speaker will tell you whether or not she chooses to accept your truth, whether she chooses to deny your truth, whether she chooses to act on your truth, or whether she chooses to even let it in. It is up to the speaker how to respond to your truth. It is up to you, my coaching friends, to speak your truth and not be afraid of the consequences.

Whenever you're going to make a powerful observation, it is to be done in a manner wherein your voice is not making any judgment, or your body language is not showing any judgment, and where you're not coming from a position of who is right or who is wrong. In coaching, we call this coming from a charge neutral position. In other words, it's perfectly fine with me, whatever it is you're doing or not doing, or whatever it is that I perceive. There's no right, there's no wrong, there's no judgment, and I can make the observation in the same way that I could observe "Oh, it's sunny out today," very natural and non-judgmental, or "Oh the American flag is red, white, and blue." Not a whole lot of excitement with my voice rising and falling - it just simply is. So it is your responsibility to simply make the observation in a natural way, without judgment.

What happens when we make a powerful observation is that we attract the speakers' attention and they get very focused and very aware of where they are in their own critical gap. They can see more definitely where they are now and where it is they want to be and what's missing as the in between. Most of us have a problem identifying or labeling what our critical gap is, what causes our critical gap, and what is holding us back from meeting our goals.

For example, I recently talked to a 20-year old, who said that she very much wanted to start her own business. When I started to ask her some questions about her business and her business vision and what it is she wanted to do, she became filled with fear and concern with money issues and a lack of self-worth. So as I listened, and by the way, this was not someone I was formally "coaching," this was just someone I was relating to in a human way as a coach, I got in-tune with her and let her know my observation about her fear and her self-esteem. So remembering that very often we don't recognize what creates our critical gap, the powerful observation can be the most important way to help someone else identify their gap and then to begin to create possibilities for moving through the gap. My final comment here is that a powerful observation, to me, is like tuning in the dial on a radio; it's getting an extremely clear frequency about where I am today and what actions are required that will allow me to move forward. So powerful observations are incredible ways to bring out the other person's truth by hearing what you observe as a truth, and being willing to share your own truth with another human being.

Let's listen in on another client session to further understand this principle:

Coach: *So, can we shift our focus to look at how you can be a great doctor? My observation is that what you're really wanting is to be a Doctor, and that you're not wanting to be the manager and operator of a business.*

Client: You mean like, maybe I can find somebody to do the practice management side of it?

Coach: Sure, you could look at that.

Client: I could outsource a lot of the business stuff.

Let's listen in on yet another session:

Client: My wife, well things are crazy. I don't believe all the things that she doesn't do. Forget leaving caps off the toothpaste, I can tolerate that; she leaves clothes on the floor, she sometimes doesn't feel like working and doesn't do things, and she doesn't have an interest in going out. I don't know what to do here. I'm at my wit's end here.

Coach: Have you had direct communication with her about your feelings?

Client: I try to tell her what she should be doing.

Coach: Ah! But I just heard you say that you are telling her what she should be doing.

Client: Well, yeah, because that's. . .

Coach: That's what?

Client: That's. . . that's. . . well, there are things that she should do. Things we all need to be doing.

Coach: So, this is the world according to you, right?

Client: Well, yes. I don't think you should drop your clothes on the floor.

Coach: So, you're coming with a certain set of beliefs and expectations.

Client: Well, yeah, that's how I was raised, to pick up your clothes and put them in the laundry and stuff like that.

Coach: Could it be that she's coming with a different set of expectations and perhaps raised in a different way?

Client: I guess.

Coach: You guess?

Client: I guess she was; I mean, obviously.

Coach: It sounds to me like you've gone to a place today of being in what I call the "judger mode."

Client: Okay.

Coach: Where you're noticing everything that's not up to your standard and holding it in judgment right now.

Client: What do I do about it?

Coach: We can start talking about what to do about it. I just want you to really note that where you're at is a place of high judgment, and I'm not hearing the same compassion, which I know is there in your heart.

Client: Yes, but wouldn't she want to change? Wouldn't you want to be a better person and take care of things better?

Coach: Again, it's being a better person by "your" standards?

Client: Well, yeah. Okay!

HEAR WHAT I SEE; SEE WHAT I HEAR

Playwork:

1. As you listen to speakers during the next week, listen for their critical gap.
2. Think about the observation that you believe is the truth about their critical gap.
3. Jot down some of the observations that you noted.
4. With one person this week, make the observation and state it simply, plainly, and clearly.
5. Make the observation with no judgment and be willing to accept whatever the speaker says next as the speaker's truth, again holding no judgment, no argument, and with complete acceptance.

Powerful Requests

Now we have learned to make powerful observations and to ask powerful questions, and the missing link here is making powerful requests. This will sound familiar to you. To make a powerful request, you want to be in-tune with the speaker and be able to hear them at a very deep, connected level, and certainly, you should be ready to make a request that will move the other person forward, a request that is a lot bigger than the other person is ready or prepared for. And then, as always, be ready for whatever response comes back to you.

Powerful requests have a purpose, and the purpose is usually to make the other person stop and allow them time to get very clear on what's fact, what's not fact, and how they might move forward to leap through the critical gap. When a speaker chooses to act upon a powerful request, he will usually make great progress in moving forward towards the other side of the critical gap. Powerful requests are always about taking action and are always way larger than the speaker can imagine. I like to pose a powerful request that is much larger than my clients think that they can possibly do. Why? Because as human beings, we tend to put ourselves down and think we can do less instead of more, and so a powerful request is a way of saying, "I believe you can do more. I can see that you can do more. I maintain that you can do more, and I want you to do more." So, go do more!

One of my clients is a Sales Manager, and he wanted to increase the amount of contracts for his company by six. I wasn't willing to accept that he would only be able to increase it by six, because six is what he had achieved the year before, and he kept telling me he wanted to do better than that. One of his critical gaps was that he had very low self-esteem about his own abilities, but I knew in my heart, and I believed, and it was my truth that he could do way more if he would just let go and do it. So, when he said, "Well, I would like to have six new clients." I said to him, "I would like to request that you have ten new clients." This was way bigger than he envisioned, way bigger than he imagined, and it allowed him to leap forward through his critical gap, and work through his self-esteem issues as well as creating more income for himself.

Powerful requests open the door and the mind to greater possibilities, greater ideas, greater magnitude of what can be done, greater expansion, and greater vision. Whenever I make a powerful request, I know that it lets people see that I believe in them, very often more than they believe in themselves. It lets them see that I expect more of them than they expect of themselves, and that I want, and envision, and hold in my belief system for them that they will achieve what it is they want.

One of the other wonderful things about powerful requests is that they actually can make other people feel very happy, bring them a great sense of joy and delight, and put a smile on their faces. For example, many years ago, when I was starting my coaching practice and really working hard to be with my clients and still marketing to attract new clients, I was feeling great pressure about not having enough space and time just to "be." Simply, to be. And so what I decided to do was take one hour off every Friday and just take great care of myself, be it to meditate or take a walk. And I remember this brilliant coach that I was working with, who I'm honored to work with at Comprehensive Coaching U, said to me, "Terri, I want you to take off one day a week." I recall thinking he must be out of his mind, and then I got this huge grin on my face and I actually remember laughing and saying, "Wouldn't that be joyful?" So then I felt lighter about it and thought well, maybe I could do that. After that, possibilities began to open up and pretty soon, low and behold, I started to take off half days. For the last year and a half to two years now, I have taken off more than one full day a week and my business is larger and more profitable than ever before. So, thank you, Coach.

Let's listen in again on the session with our Doctor friend:

Coach: *So what I'm hearing is that you are willing to take a look at how you can have a medical practice and perhaps not be the marketing guru of getting patients. Is that right?*

Client: Well yes, because what I really want is a great medical practice. I just want to arrive in the morning and have a room full of patients to take care of and make them well.

Coach: Great! So I'd like to make some requests here, and anytime that I make a request, you can accept it, you can deny it, or we can negotiate it. Would that work for you?

Client: Okay.

Coach: Okay, great. So, the first request is that you take some time in the next couple of days and really envision, I mean deeply envision, get it in your mind, your brain, in your body, in your heart, and your gut, what it would be like to have a perfect day as a physician. Just perfect. You would be doing what you love, with your patients, you would feel like you were a wonderful doctor and were accomplishing all the things that you want to accomplish. Would you be willing to take on that request?

Client: I could. It would be a stretch from where I am now. But I would be willing to do it.

Coach: Notice that with coaching, I'm always going to request that you stretch. Are you willing to go there?

Client: I could do that.

Coach: Great! And the second request that I have is that you sit down and make a list on your computer, or in a journal, or meditate and come up with a list of all the things that are going right, day-to-day, in your work. Every single thing.

Client: I have some really good patients. I love being able to help them. I truly love being a doctor and enjoy medicine. I feel great when I've been able to help someone.

Coach: Great! I'm sure you're doing a wonderful job. I want you to really get turned on to what's going right. So my request is that you shift your focus

44

and really take some concrete time to look at what's working. Would you be willing to do that?

Client: *I suppose I could.*

Coach: *This "suppose I could"... is there something holding you back here?*

Client: *No, I just see so many problems that I don't know what to do about it.*

Coach: *Great, let's let go of the problems, that's another request. Just let it go. Let it go to the Universe for right now and let's just put our focus for right now on what's working. We'll deal with the other stuff. You're willing to do that?*

Client: *Okay.*

Coach: *Great.*

THE POWER OF REQUESTS

Playwork:

1. As you listen to speakers this week, hear their critical gaps.
2. Create a request that will help them move closer to the other side of the gap or to achieve what it is that they want or to handle whatever has come up.
3. Hold no attachment or judgment whether they accept or deny your request – either one is fine and completely up to them.

So here you have some incredible tools to make you a really powerful coach. We've talked about powerful questions, powerful observations, and powerful requests. Sometimes it's a little scary to think about using these tools, but I can assure you that if you want to bring richness into your life and into the lives of others, these tools will allow for deeper understanding and the ability to want for other people so much more than they can see for themselves. Does it take courage to be a powerful coach? You bet it does! It's okay to be willing to be wrong, to be non-judgmental, and to be willing to really want to celebrate other people achieving more then they ever thought possible. Enjoy the powerful questions, observations, and requests, and think about how that works for you in your own life. Whenever I'm stuck, I turn within and ask myself, what would be a request that I could make of myself right now, that might cause me some discomfort, yet at the same time, allow me to make a huge leap and a huge gain.

4

Bodybuilding, Mind building, Spirit building

You're probably already recognizing that by learning coaching tools, you will not only be helping to create a better world and a better environment for the people you come in contact with everyday, but one of the greatest benefits of becoming a coach, either as a professional or as a private individual is that you will begin to pick up skills that will help you to evolve and grow and develop beyond who you currently are.

I tell people who take our Coach Training Program at Comprehensive Coaching U that it doesn't matter to me whether they decide to become a professional coach. What does matter to me is that they use the tools in their way of being a human. I know, as coaches, if we focus on the goodness in other people and the strengths that other people have, we'll create better life experiences for everyone on the planet and also for ourselves.

I want to talk here about relationships. Anytime we communicate with someone, we're in a relationship. When I earned my Master of Science Degree as a Speech-Language Pathologist, I felt that I was a communication expert. I will say, however, that when I became a coach, and over the years through coaching my clients, I have recognized that I know more about communication now because of the skills I have learned as a coach than I did as a Speech-Language Pathologist. It is essential to me that other people have these same tools; that's why I'm putting them here in this book; that's why I do training and speaking about them; and that's one of the reasons that Comprehensive Coaching U exists. We, as human beings, want relationships, need relationships, and thrive on relationships, and relationships are built on our way of being and our way of communicating.

Since most of us have problems even knowing ourselves, how can we help other people in the world when we're not clear what our own vision is, what our strengths are, and what our critical gaps are? It's simple, if you hold the belief that each person is a good person, who has his or her own way of being, and you hold no judgment about whose way of being is best, right, or wrong, and simply accept them as they are. I believe that as we build relationships, we can focus on building other people's self-esteem and self-image, and at the same time, focus on improving our own.

So as we develop ourselves, we will know ourselves more; we'll have a better view of who we are; we'll eliminate a lot of our disbeliefs about ourselves; we'll stop putting ourselves down; we'll create a wonderful way of being that gives us a big picture of our life or creates a flow of energy; we'll see possibilities; we'll feel peaceful; we'll feel optimistic; we'll feel joy; and one of my most important words is that we will have more fun. So what comes from being coach-like? I'll tell you; it's very simple. You have a more positive attitude because you're not dwelling on the negatives of other people. I experience my life by choice and by believing that other people are good. I accept who other people are, and as a human being, I take great joy and delight in working with other people, to see them achieve their goals, to grow as individuals, to find all the wonderful talents, gifts, and skills that they have, and of course, to create more fun in their own lives.

So you already know that you're going to be very tuned into other people from now on and you're going to really hear what they believe, what they want, and you're going to always listen so that you can identify their critical gap and really understand what's missing for them. Use these same tools for yourself, understand yourself better, and know what will move you forward and what your own critical gap is.

We all need a better understanding of who we are as human beings and a greater sense of self. We all share similar wants of being on this planet. We come to this planet in wanting to be happy and wanting to feel good and wanting success and wanting to be valued and honored. So what you are going to do to build other people up is to hold the belief that each person is absolutely perfect, right here, right now, in whatever way, shape, or form they are. They are right where they are supposed to be, everything is the way it's supposed to be for them, and everything that they want, they have the ability to have. Now you may start thinking, "How will that apply if someone is coming to me whose family member has just been diagnosed with cancer, or who has a son or a daughter who has Down Syndrome, or who has just suffered a tragedy in their family or loss of a loved one?" If we believe that these are life lessons and if we believe that things just are the way they are for some divine reason and some purpose, then it's a whole lot easier to focus on what we are learning and how we can move forward. So when I hear people talk about being unhappy, or not being loved enough, or feeling very stressed, or not having a spouse that is supportive, or having all kinds of fears about the future, or complaints about their boss, or problems with their children, I simply refocus and say, "Well what is working for you? What is okay today? What is perfect today? Is the fact that you woke up this morning, perfect? Is the fact that the sun came out perfect? Is the fact that you were able to get through breakfast perfect?" Something is always perfect. As human beings, we tend to focus so much on what is wrong versus what is right. As the coach, you're going to put your focus on what is right for other people and what is right for you. Not what is wrong and what was wrong and all the wrongs that have been done against you. This is a big shift for most people; most of us like to talk about problems and what isn't working. So I'll bear my soul to you here and tell you that for many years, as an executive in corporate America, I was really great at identifying all the problems. This isn't working, that's not working, this employee's no good, the revenues are down, productivity is down, my car phone isn't working, I have too many e-mails, too many voicemails, I have too long to commute to work, the company isn't treating the employees right, and on and on.

The way I operate my business entities now is that I believe that everything is perfect. So, knowing that one of my companies is a virtual university, Comprehensive Coaching U, you might imagine that I would be greatly distressed to find out that for whatever reason, my Website disappeared off the face of the planet for 24 hours. I don't know where it was, but anyone who tried to get there got an error message saying the site did not exist or was not responding. I could have focused on what was wrong. Well, what was wrong was we had just done a large advertising campaign and had quite a few ads running, and I had recently done many interviews, and been on the radio, and written up in the newspapers. Wow! All that work. Our Website address was given out, but no one could find us. Now what? I didn't choose to focus on what was wrong; instead I began to ask, "So what is working?" And I began to say that what is working is that we did have a lot of ads and we have had the opportunity to get a lot of information out there, and we have had some really great opportunities in the print and media, and many people will remember our Website and will call us back somewhere along the line. So what else is working? What's working is at least I know our Website is not working, and what else is working is that by tomorrow our Website will probably be working again and what's working is I was able to get the Webmaster right on the phone and I know it'll be fixed. As soon as I changed my focus and changed my energy, I began to have a different experience on the planet. I just simply don't allow myself to get taken down by outside circumstances, nor do I do that to other people. Many years ago, I heard motivational speaker, Zig Ziglar, speaking about a term that he called "snioping." What I got from this was that snioping is being subjective to the negative influences of other people. What I've taken from that over the years is that I was a snioper. I would bring other people down by telling them all the things that weren't working and what was wrong and I would spend a lot of energy around that. I also found I attracted a lot more people who snioped me; I would come to work feeling motivated and energized and then they would tell me all the things that were wrong or that weren't working. As soon as I was able to shift and get very clearly focused and put my energy around spending time with people who were not in a snioping mode and not allowing other people to bring me down, my experience on this planet became one of joy and delight, each day, every day, and you can create that for yourself, if you choose to. You absolutely choose how you want to experience your life on this earth.

So now we're absolutely listening to other people, and we're hearing what gets in the way, what is blocking their energy, what is causing their behaviors to be stuck, and we're hearing this in ourselves. We're not judging right or wrong, we're simply understanding that things come up which get in our way as human beings, and that it's just an amazing miracle that we have everything we need today, here on this planet. Instead of focusing on what's missing, and what we are lacking, and what we don't have, and what we'd like to have but we can never have, we begin to change the focus, and we can do that for other people too.

WHAT IS WORKING?

Playwork: Looking for What's Right

1. Write down everything today that is working for you, everything that is going right, everything that makes today perfect, and that you know you are precisely where you are supposed to be today.
2. Note what lessons you have learned from your experiences today. Even the things you didn't think were perfect, notice how they are perfect and how they have given you a great gift, or a gift you can use in the future.
3. Listen carefully to one person today and hear what gets in their way of who they are and what they want.

There are certain building blocks that will help in your relationships with other people to develop and grow. One is the basic premise of trust. Although it may seem like something that we automatically do, this is a different type of trust and belief than we typically have in our experiences. It is trust of believing in who the other person is and their greatness and in really seeing their full potential to accomplish whatever they may choose. Another building block is the ability to communicate what you believe for the other person. Sometimes we see things in other people, or believe things about them, or envision their greatness, but we don't express that. This is a way of telling other people what we see about them, what we believe about them, and what excites us about who they are, and what their natural gifts and talents are that they bring to this universe. I'd like you to think about communicating, on a regular basis, what you see in other people that's great, what you expect of other people, and the vision that you hold for other people. We're very good, as human beings, at telling other people what's wrong with them, what they haven't done right, what their faults are, why we don't think they'll achieve something, and why some things are not a good idea. Coaches communicate a world of possibility and potential for other people and holding a vision for them that they can achieve anything, and that you really have belief and faith in who they are and what they can do.

There's a story about the bumblebee that I use often when addressing audiences. Aerodynamically, bumblebees are not supposed to be able to fly. It defies science and it defies logic. However, we see bumblebees out there flying around every single day. Why is that? I believe it's because nobody ever told the bumblebee that they're not supposed to be able to fly. They never heard that they can't fly and so they just go ahead and fly. What I'm getting at here is that if we really believe in other people and believe that they can do the unexpected and achieve the unachievable, then their goals and who they are as human beings makes them unstoppable. So this is about holding the vision of greatness for other people.

Something else that we are not particularly good at as human beings is letting people know how right they are and really noticing what's working about them, what we appreciate about them, what we honor about them, and what we respect about them. Once again, we're very well trained in telling people what's wrong about them, how they look, how they act, how they make us feel, etc. As a coach, it is important to always honor and recognize and affirm other people, and again, to speak to them about their greatness and what you see and what you appreciate about them and the great gifts that they bring and how valuable those are to you and to the rest of the human experience.

We're also very good, as human beings, at telling people what's wrong, what's going to be wrong, how bad things are, how bad things can be, and generally discouraging other people. When I was ready to leave corporate America at a high six-figure income, people told me not to do it. "You won't be able to make any money, it's really hard to start your own business, you should be glad you have this great job, you're being ungrateful." I could go on and on with the stories of discouragement that people told me. In my own heart and my own head, I tuned them out and found a coach who offered me encouragement, offered me belief, told me that my goals were reachable, achievable, really held for me that I could achieve them, meet them, and exceed them. Let's shift our focus on telling people how things aren't working and why it's not going to work and why things are a bad idea to now tell them how excited we are for them, for their possibilities, and let's give them hope and optimism.

I think you're probably getting the gist here that one of the basic building blocks of being a great coach is coming from a positive belief and really helping people achieve what it is they want to achieve and believing and envisioning that others are capable beyond the abilities that they can even see for themselves.

One of the things that you can focus on, as you're relating to other people day to day, is what it is in their life that might be working really well for them. Again, our search to find what is working in other people's lives helps them shift their focus to what is working. So what is it that people already have in their experience that is working well for them: is it their friends, is it their family, is it their business, is it love, or is it recognition? One of the things you'll be listening for is what people already have in their experience that's working and what could be enhanced to work even better and create better experiences. For example, you might hear that someone feels like they're doing okay financially, so that's working, but wouldn't it be great if they could do even better financially? Or you might hear somebody talking about how well their business is going and then finding that it could be doing more, could be doing better, and so again, helping to take it to the next level.

At this time you might be asking, "So why should I be helping everybody else and offering this information to everybody else? I have my own self to take care of." My belief and what I've seen in my experience in coaching and training thousands of people around the world is that if we better ourselves, and we become better people, and we really take great care to treat other people with coach-like manners and coach-like respect and coach-like integrity and dignity, then we elevate everyone's experience, especially our own.

What's also important is helping other people to understand that life is just a wonderful journey, that it has its ups and its downs, that things change and the past will be different than the present, the future will look different than we could ever anticipate, and that's just the way life is and the way we experience life. It's not about having a perfect life and being a perfectionist, it's just about experiencing life, the ups, the downs, and the bumps, and really understanding that we'll have our highs and our lows, good emotions, not so good emotions, good experiences, not so good experiences and again, these are just the ebbs and flows that are natural in our lifetime. Another way that I like to enhance the experience for other people is to really understand their goals and their big picture and really try to hold the goal for them. What I mean by that is if someone says that they really want to find a new career and that they are going on job interviews and putting a lot of resumes out there and going through the paper and whatever else they might be doing, then I will also envision that goal with them. I'll want it, I'll believe in it, and actually, I'll believe in it in a bigger way. The way I do it in a bigger way is I challenge, you've heard that before, really challenge the other person to make the goal bigger, to expand the goal, because I can usually see it bigger, faster, and easier. Why can I see it bigger, faster, easier? It's not because I'm clairvoyant; it's not because I have any special skills; it comes from this basic building block of carrying a strong belief in other people.

It's also important to allow other people to enjoy their successes, and their accomplishments, and whenever they achieve a goal, big, small, or in between medium, to honor them for that, to celebrate with them. I talked to a friend of mine who had lost 30 pounds recently and I was just so excited for her; she looked great and I congratulated her, but instead of taking in the compliment, the first thing she said was, "Well, I still have a long way to go; I still want to lose 20 more. It's still going to be another year." So she wasn't letting it in. It's time to let in the celebration, to stand up and cheer and say, "Hey, this is great. I celebrate with you. I recognize you," and this is an important part of being a coach in the world with friends, family, neighbors, children, parents, and whoever else crosses your path. Look around at all the people in your environment and look for ways to celebrate them, their greatness, their accomplishments, and not to bring them down.

5

Evolving Others

With the coaching background that you have, it'll be important for you to see how to begin to weave this together in a way that really supports and helps other people to evolve and to develop to an even greater level of being.

It's impossible to grow other people, to help other people, and to coach other people, unless we've done some of this work on ourselves. Again, as you are going through this material and as you're experiencing the world of coaching, keep very focused on the fact that this experience, coaching, learning to be a coach, becoming a coach, and learning coaching tools, doesn't only benefit the way you're going to be with other people and enjoy your own experience with other people, it has the selfishly wonderful benefit of allowing you to be in a different place, in a different space, and in a different way with yourself.

Coaches find that they have less emotional ups and downs, less emotional judgment, less baggage, less issues, greater happiness, more effortless lives, they work less and make a lot more money, and that they have an encouraging, rewarding experience as people. What are some things that are important for you to be as a coach? First, it's being non-judgmental. It's to be accepting of all people and all things. Second, is to recognize that we're not trying to cure, fix, or change anybody into becoming someone that they are not. Third, is to listen to understand where people are, again without judgment, just with full and complete recognition; a willingness to be completely tuned in and emotionally charge free so that you can hear, tune in, and let in other people's experiences. We then listen for *what's up* with the other person, what their views are, what their goals are, what their critical gap might be that's holding them back. We're listening for their greatness, we're listening for ways that perhaps we can help them grow and leap forward, while holding the vision of their greatness as a human being and as someone we want to have a wonderful experience with on the planet.

As we begin to really get in touch with other people and with where they are and where they want to be, we're going to notice that many times people have goals without a sense of why they want to achieve them, or even how they want to achieve them. As you listen to other people's goals, dreams, wishes, and wants, try to listen for why they want to achieve these goals and how these goals would change them or their life, and how that might improve their experience. We won't achieve goals if the goal isn't something we passionately desire and want and work towards everyday.

I coached a client recently who said that he wanted to sell his home and he wanted to build a log cabin. Yet every week when we talked, he wasn't putting his home up for sale, he wasn't getting his home ready to put up for sale, he wasn't looking into where to build a log cabin, or how to build one, or the property for a log cabin. So it became very evident to me that this wasn't really his goal, there wasn't a huge desire here, but there didn't need to be any guilt; we could just drop the goal and move along to something that the client really wanted.

Again, when we're listening as coaches, we are also listening to hold a bigger goal, a bigger vision to expand the goal. I've had clients come to me who say that they want to begin a business and they would like to make $3,000 a month. I immediately raise the goal, raise the bar, go for more, so that people get an opportunity to see that somebody else believes in them and believes that the goal could be bigger. Don't choose a goal that is so out of whack that you can't believe it for the other person and they can't believe it for themselves. Simply see how you can help them make the goal a little bit bigger, a little bit higher, a little bit more passionate, a little bit more exciting, and a little bit more challenging. That's what we want our life experiences to be about.

GOALS ARE GOLDEN

Playwork:

1. Listen carefully to those in your life and find out what their burning, passionate goals are.
2. Write down how you might expand each goal for each of those persons.
3. Suggest to one or more of the people that you see them achieving a bigger goal and that you will hold that vision for them.

As you sense that people really want to grow and achieve their goals and have a better existence on the planet, you can begin to use more coaching tools with them. You can go a little bit higher and ask for things that are bigger, bigger goals, a request that may feel really difficult, and really out there. One of the things that I use as a coach is asking for even bigger, different behaviors. You can also ask people to achieve more in a shorter space of time to get them to move faster.

I believe that when people hire coaches, they do so because they really want to achieve results and they know that a coach who's not attached to the outcome of what occurs can really hold the vision and get them to be accountable, to achieve the results they couldn't get on their own. Here is an example for you. I know that this book would have been another year in the making had I not had the wonderful experience of working with my publisher, Jim Donovan, who coached me and made me spring into action when he set the date that the book would be published. So Jim really held out for me that he saw a bigger result and thought that it could be achieved, and then he held me accountable, and boy, do I thank him for that!

I want to also mention that frequently as we talk with other people, we want to really focus our attention on what's most important for them. Sometimes, when something significant has occurred in their lives, they want to talk about it at great detail. They want to dwell on it and it's hard for them to get off the topic. When I listen to someone in that situation, I try to really be with them, stand in their shoes, experience what they are experiencing, and then I try to guide them to release the emotion and some of the feelings they are having so that they can move off from it and begin to have a new experience, ask themselves different questions, and get some different answers for themselves.

I was coaching a couple just the other day, who had had a significant argument, and you could hear in their voices they were both angry and both hurting. Both wanted to talk about their experience and how wrong the other person was and how they were feeling, and I certainly allowed them to do that so that I could stand in their shoes, I could be with them, and I could fully hear them. As their coach, it's important to me that they come to a place of being able to satisfy the emotion and really begin to just look at what came up for them around that issue. What is the underlying issue? What is this really about? Why did this push their buttons so much? Turn it more into learning about them. Why is it that this set them off? Why is it that it felt this way to them? Not, let's make the other person wrong. This coaching tool is a way of getting people to change their way of looking at things, it's getting people to begin to see things from another person's perspective and to not be as attached to being right. So as you listen to people and you hear that they are emotionally charged, stand with them in their shoes, allow them to get their venting done and then see how you can gently, lovingly, shift them to begin to release, let go, so that they can move on.

Part of what I'm doing here is helping people change the view or change their point-of-view and their reference, and not selling them on the fact that the other person was right, or that they might even want to agree with the other person. I simply want them to release, let it go and just understand why that triggered something for them. Why did that really get under their skin, because really, it's about their reaction. If we could all understand that when somebody pushes our buttons, upsets us, or says something that makes us angry, it's really something about us. It's something about our reaction, because that could happen to another person and another person could think, "Big deal, who cares!" But it's us that decided to take it seriously. I say "decided" because it really is a choice. Let's say I am doing a speaking engagement and you're in the audience, and you don't like the way I present and you fill out an evaluation, "Oh she's the worst speaker I ever heard. I don't like her. I don't like what she has to say. She's short." Whatever you might say, I read it and go, "Okay, that's about them. Boy, they are carrying a lot of anger. I guess they don't like short people." It's all about the other person. I don't choose to let it be about me.

6

Helping Others Achieve Goals

We all have some type of goals. Often, when I ask young children what their goals are, they say they don't have any. I begin to break it down for them. Do you want to wake-up in the morning? Do you want to go to school? Do you want to eat ice cream? Do you want a puppy? Do you want to be a lawyer? Do you want to drive a car? From there they usually start talking about things that they want. I believe we all have goals. I sometimes believe we think our goals aren't goals because they seem to be small. And I believe, sometimes, that some of us have goals that are so big, we're afraid to share them with anyone. I believe that each person has a goal. You have a goal in reading this book. I don't know if you're reading this book because you want to be a coach, are in the profession of coaching, or if it's because you're planning to hire a coach, or perhaps you hired a coach who asked you to read the book, or perhaps you're a parent, a teacher, a grandparent, a sibling, or in a relationship, or in a business environment. You have a goal in reading this book. You have the intention of getting something that you want from this book. I believe that if you are very focused on what it is you want, you will get it.

We've all heard about goal setting. *You can't get there without a map. You need to plan your success. You need a blueprint for your success.* Do I agree with that? Yes, you need to really have clarity about the goals you want to achieve and why you want to achieve them and then, how you're going to get there. I don't like to spend a lot of time and energy or go into detail when working on my own personal goals. I like to do a very simple goal plan, which allows me to really make a commitment towards a goal, to really understand why I want that goal, why that's really important to me and is a burning desire for me. If I were able to achieve my goal, what would that look like? How would that feel? What would the emotions be that would occur for me, the feelings that would arise for me? What are the things that I would get from my goal? I also like to have some sense of when I'm going to achieve this and some method of keeping track or understanding the essence of time frames that I want. For each goal that I have, whether it be a financial goal, a business goal, a relationship goal, a personal goal, a social goal, a spiritual goal, or a community goal, etc., I also think about the various resources that I will need to bring this goal into reality. Is it going to take a lot of energy? Am I going to spend a lot of emotion? Am I going to need some financial resources? Am I going to need a network of people? Am I going to need some special skills? Am I going to need some special training?

For everything that you have a burning desire for in your life, it's important to set some goals around those burning desires.

MY DESIRE IS ON FIRE

Playwork:

1. Create a list of goals in each area of your life that are burning, that you truly do not want to leave the planet, today, tomorrow, or 50 years from now without achieving.
2. If you were going to leave the planet 30 days from now, which of your goals is the one that you absolutely do not want to leave incomplete?
3. Write down that goal and then write down why you want it, how it will change your life, all the feelings and emotions associated with achieving this goal, your timeframes for achieving the goal, the steps that you need to take to achieve the goal, and the resources that you will need to achieve the goal.
4. Take some action today towards moving forward to achieve your goal.
5. Plan to take action in some fashion every day, almost like taking a multi-vitamin. Something that will allow you to experience getting closer to your goal, each day and every day.

7

The Many Truths

We use the word "truth" a lot and talk about being open and being honest and being truthful as people. I will tell you that there are many different kinds of truths that we talk about in coaching. I mean, certainly, you have your own truth about how you're experiencing your day and I have my truth about how I'm experiencing my day, and yours is perfectly true for you and mine is perfectly true for me. What we perceive is what we believe and is, therefore, what we hold as our own truth. Might our truths differ? Absolutely. We're also taught, in many cases, that we shouldn't share our truth or state our truth or we should actually hide the truth.

So when someone approaches you and says, "Hey do you like my new haircut?" and you're thinking, "Boy, that looks pretty bad," we go through this questioning of "Do I tell them *the* truth?" For our purposes, I'm going to define truth as something that is objective and based on data. An example is today is January the 24th. It's not debatable, it just is. Each person that you come in contact with will have their own truth, their own perceptions, their own beliefs. Sometimes it includes the data that is true and very often it includes their own feelings, their own emotions, opinions, judgments, values, and view of looking at the world, which is usually based upon their past experiences. I'm going to ask you to listen to other people and listen for what their truth is. This is different. We typically listen and then we want to tell everybody what our truth is and want to get everybody to believe what our truth is.

For example, imagine that your teenage son or daughter got a "D" on their report card in science and their truth is "The teacher doesn't like me." How do we get at really understanding their truth and how their truth came to be and why their truth is? The way to do it is by using coaching tools and really trying to listen, be very tuned in, use powerful questions, make powerful observations, use powerful requests, and really try to understand what is the root cause or the issue here, and see if there is a way that we can help your son or daughter to leap forward. So it is important to always be listening for somebody else's truth, because their truth is how they're experiencing their life. I listen without judgment to whatever a client tells me, or whatever a friend, family member, neighbor, or anyone in my experience tells me. And then I ask questions to try to really understand what their truth is, why that's their truth, again without holding judgment, just to see if I can help them see different perspectives. As I'm listening, I'm certainly going to have my own truth. My truth is based on the same things; it's based on my experiences in life, what's happened to me in the past, my values, judgments, and emotions, based on my feelings. I'm always going to have something that I believe as someone else is talking to me. While I'm listening in a non-judgmental way, there are still going to be things that I notice in the process of listening, and I also listen for fictional, or data based, truth, and whenever I am not clear on the data or the facts, that's where I'm going to really try and find out what and where the truth is for the other person. I'm also not afraid to share my truths with other people and to really tell what my truth is, which is to simply say, "You know, this is what comes up for me," or "This is what I think," or "Here is my opinion," or "This is what I'm thinking and if that works for you, fine, and if not just let it be."

This takes guts, it takes practice, and it takes you to another level of being. We are trained, we are taught to hold back, to not tell the truth, to stay away from being truthful, to not hurt people. What I find is that when we stay away from the truth, we actually hurt people more and cause people more pain. So as I listen to other people talk, I may tell them what I hear that is true and just allow them to try it on. They can reject what I hear, or they can just tell me it's absolutely not their truth. For an example, I had a family member tell me that she was not upset by something that had happened, yet she looked upset, sounded upset, acted upset, and I'm sure, this was making other people in the room upset. I proceeded to say, "I would like you to know that my observation is that you appear to be upset and I just wanted to share that with you. If it's not true for you just let me know."

That's different, we typically don't do that, we typically hold back and so when you stand up and speak your truth in a non-judgmental, honest, respectful way, very often people will be taken back a little bit just because it is new. As you begin to speak your truth more and more, you'll see that other people respect it, appreciate it, and honor you, and thank you for speaking your truth. When listening to other people and really listening for their truth, always make sure that you're holding other people as valuable and important and that you're leaving behind any attachment, preconceived notion, or judgment. Let people know that no matter what their truth is, you accept them, you feel great about them, you respect them, and it just simply doesn't matter to you what their truth is.

Again, here is another real life example. I have a close friend who is in a relationship with another woman, and who for some reason wants us all to believe that she is heterosexual. I have no judgment about homosexual, heterosexual, bisexual, that's completely up to you and how you want to experience your life on this planet. As I noticed she was not speaking her truth, and she was disguising her truth, I simply created a very safe place, an environment, and told her that I was non-judgmental in anything that came up for her and any of my friends, that I respected her, that I loved her, that I cared about who she was, and that I had a truth to share with her, and it was my truth, and if it did not ring true for her, she could give me some clarity around that. This immediately opened up the door for our conversation, brought us to a closer level, allowed her to feel more comfortable sharing this with me, and then later, with other people.

8

Play Yourself Happy

One of the things that I want most in my life is to have fun and to play. I find many people take life very seriously, take their experiences very seriously, take their relationships seriously, and their work seriously, and I'm here to tell you that you can have a wonderful life, a rewarding life, a fulfilling life, and you can simply and joyfully play yourself happy. I envision a world where we're each not only playing ourselves happy, we're contributing to other people experiencing life in the same way, with great happiness and a playful spirit. So let's think back to being children and running around in the playground and laughing, eating ice cream, going to the beach for the first time, catching fireflies, and rolling in the snow. Let's remember all the joyful things that we do as children and how light we feel and how we run and we laugh and we're silly and we don't care if anybody looks at us, and we imagine, we make up, we pretend, we're happy and joyful.

That's how I experience my life, that's how my clients have begun to experience their lives, and if you're ready, it's now your turn, not only to experience your life this way, but to begin to help other people that you know experience their life with more joy and more sense of play.

As we become adults we simply forget what it's like to be with toys and to use toys and to play games, and to laugh, and to smile, and to imagine. We're so concerned about how other people will see us and perceive us and the right way of being, that we cover up our inner laughter, our inner joy, the silly things that we have enjoyed doing.

THE PLAYGROUND OF LIFE

Playwork:

1. Spend some time with a child, a young child, this week, either watching them, speaking with them, playing with them, painting with them, reading to them, or just sitting and laughing with them.

2. Do something completely out of character and childish this week.

3. Go buy a silly toy, could be a yo-yo or a stuffed animal- my favorite is my Furby. Many of my clients have enjoyed Mr. Potato Head, Pick-up Sticks, Minnie & Mickey Mouse, and so on.

4. Find a way of making a heavy situation become light by acting childlike, or by putting yourself into the mode of "How would I respond to this if I were a child?"

Enjoy and delight and relish in the fact that you can be playful. You can have fun. You're allowed to and it will contribute to your experience as a human being. Give other people permission to laugh; laugh with them. Take your employees to the park and have a picnic and have potato sack races. Put a clown's nose on in the car and wave to other people as you drive around. Share humorous stories with your friends. Think of all the ways that you can play games, have fun, be childlike, enjoy, imagine and create, and do that with the other people that you come in contact with everyday.

9

Change

Ever heard the expression that "the only constant is change"? That's really what our life is about; it's about making changes, learning, growing, experiencing our life's journey through ebbs and flows and up and downs and many kinds of changes. Some of the changes may be joyful and fun and energetic, and some may feel heavy and bring sadness and longing. If we take into account that we're constantly changing and that the people around us are also changing and evolving and growing and that their life experiences and what shows up for them everyday is changing, evolving and growing, then it'll be easier for us to act in a coach-like manner in guiding and assisting other people to move through change with less effort and to move at a faster pace. Most of us are not that comfortable with the word "change." We simply don't like it. We prefer things to go along just the way they are and not have to deal with any ups and downs or challenges that come before us. But it's inevitable. As I said, it's just a part of our experience, and it's just something that we're going to have to deal with and go through. Once we understand that everybody in our life experience will be changing and their lives will also be changing, then we'll be coming from a better place in understanding how to relate to them.

Change happens for many reasons and in many different ways. Sometimes change happens because something has occurred that causes the change: someone has been downsized, someone has become ill, someone has moved, or someone has a huge goal and they have to make some changes to get there. Sometimes change comes from thinking that something is going to happen or come in the future like "I may be downsized." Or "We're planning on moving." Or "I maybe leaving my life partner." And so we begin to make some changes to get ready and to be prepared. Sometimes change comes and we're not even sure how we're doing it, why we're changing, but all of a sudden we're finding we just are, that the way things hit us are different, the way we respond is different, the way we feel is different, things that made us happy in the past, just aren't making us as happy anymore.

If we come from the premise that our lives evolve and change, then we can understand that change is normal for us, for our friends, family, children, loved ones, employees, employers and on and on. I hold the belief that our lives will be better because of change, and that sometimes, being forced to make changes or going through changes is very difficult and unpleasant and may cause some sadness, but I truly believe that it's just a part of our existence, a part of the way we come to experience our lives. How can you help other people make changes, and in what areas do other people want to make changes? It's important to really listen again to the people you are experiencing to understand who they really are. What's important to them, what is it they want? Is there something in the way that might be blocking what they want, and do they need to make some changes to achieve that? For example, if I really want to be a thin person, I'm probably going to have to change the basic foundation of the way that I eat, and my eating framework is going to have to shift. Or it may be that I'm going to change and I'm going to use more of my entrepreneur tools versus being an employee. So, as I'm listening and noticing someone in my life experience that I care about, wanting to make some changes in their profession or in their business, I really want to understand why it's important for them, what's important for them, and how they see the change as being important in their lives. Another type of change that people make is wanting to give up a particular habit or pattern that they have had in their lives. It could even be that they want to lose weight, or they want to have a relationship that's more rewarding, or it could be they want to quit smoking, or maybe it could be they want to approach their lives differently with less effort and more joy.

What happens is that change becomes a scary place for most human beings. We are afraid that change is somehow going to be bad. It's unknown, so we're not sure of the outcome and we feel out of control when change is upon us. You can help yourself and other people understand change, and to really understand the basic premise of coaching is that all people are changing, want to change, or may have a desire to change. Again, you can be a coach to everyone and anyone that you experience if you choose to really be tuned in to how to help people work through change. Often people don't even realize that they are going through change. I have a friend who no longer seemed happy in her marriage and talked at length about that. It appeared to me that the change was that she, herself, had changed in many ways. She had higher self-esteem, higher goals, and very different values than her husband of 10 years. And so the first step for me in being her friend and being her coach was to simply stand and recognize that she was changing, and that change was occurring, and then help her recognize that the change was happening. Sometimes it takes people a long time to change because they get stuck in the past and hold on to things that happened in the past and they feel sadness or a lot of emotion about releasing the past. I had this come up for myself when I made the decision to no longer have a business associate that I was collaborating with at the time. And while it was very difficult, I recognized that I had changed, I had grown, and this relationship was no longer serving me or serving my business entity. It was very difficult to share that information, because again, I didn't want to hurt the other person's feelings. There was some sadness because I cared deeply for the other person; I didn't want to bring up a lot of emotion, and so, until I could really recognize that I wanted to move ahead and recognize that this was a very major and important goal for me, I couldn't untangle the past experiences and emotions. Where being a coach helped me a lot, was to enable me to stand and recognize what was challenging me about wanting to make this change and what was holding me back from making the change. It was very simply that I was remembering the past of, "Oh, it was this way. It could have been this way. Wasn't that nice? Wasn't that fun?" and then, finally saying that I wanted to release that, allowed me to make change much more quickly and in a much happier way.

So I want you to be very focused on changes that are occurring for you, changes that occur for you by reading this book, by experiencing coaching, by being trained as a coach, by using coaching techniques with your children or your family or your friends or your employees or anything else that comes up for you in your life experience. I also want you to wear a second hat, which involves starting to really look at other people and see what's happening for them that might involve change, be it in their job, or their own identification of who they are, or their goals, or in their relationships. What is concerning other people about change? All of us move through change at different speeds and react differently to different kinds of change, and again, I hold no judgment here, just understand that this is part of our life experience. This is what happens for us on this planet, and we can support other people by just being non-judgmental, by being supportive, and helping them recognize the changes and identifying what the changes are. How do you know if you are able to help other people through change, particularly if you're not a change agent yourself and you move slowly through change? My answer here is that every time we go through a change, or help somebody else go through a change, we learn so many valuable life lessons that help us grow and develop and that we can then share with other people. So change is all about moving through it faster with greater ease, acknowledging that it's just a part of our existence. Our role, since all of us are going to be wearing coaching hats, is to help other people get acclimated to change and experience change with more joy and more lightness through what we call coaching.

Now you're ready for the specifics on how to help yourself and other people through change. It may sound silly to say that the first step is to recognize what the change is that the other person wants or is moving towards. Same for yourself, what is the change you want; what's the result you want as a result of reading this book? I like to ask other people to tell me about what they see changing and how they see it changing, and more importantly, what the feelings and emotions, and the results, and the experiences will be once they've moved through change. Sometimes, I think we forget when we're going through change that not everything will change and that we can still hold on to some wonderful things from the past, if we so choose. For an example, one of my clients was promoted from being a Staff Physical Therapist to being the Department Manager of the Physical Therapy Department at a hospital. He was so afraid that when he changed and became the Manager, he would lose his friends, become a "bossy" type person, be mean, non-caring and unconcerned, and he was really petrified of what was going to occur. I held for him the belief, which was strong for me, that none of that would happen, because he was still him. And that while he would be wearing a different hat, and while he would be doing a different job, he would still be the same person with the same values and the same friends and the same relationships.

I talk a lot in this book about how to help other people really see how great they are and identify their strengths, talents, and values. Remembering that everyone is going through change and that as you're going to wear a coaching hat, you're going to help people move through change with more ease, more fun, and more finesse, keep in mind that you're always holding the vision and the view of being non-judgmental and seeing the wonderful values, talents, skills, and traits, that other people possess.

I look at myself in this light as a guide. A guide who can achieve many things for herself and can guide other people to achieve many things for themselves. So, as a guide, I want to really listen and get connected with other people and understand what's up for them and where they see change or where they need change and then to relay back to them, with my language and with my empathy, some of the things that might help them move through change while letting them feel more of a sense of control in going through change. Since I believe each person is great and unique and special and wonderful just as they are, I believe that as we change and develop and grow and have more life experiences, these will just strengthen our greatness and our talents and our sense of who we are. Because change sometimes takes a long time and sometimes we get caught up in change or stuck in change, I like to help everyone in my environment, simply by letting them know that I'm here for them, that I support them, that I care about them, and that no matter what is happening in the change cycle of their life experience, I'm here to be with them and to celebrate with them and to honor them, and if they need some help, if they're stuck, then I can help them get some momentum, and that this is my role. It's my role whether they're paying me to be their coach, or whether I'm in a relationship with them simply as their friend, their aunt, their sister, their daughter, their spouse, their lover, or their employer, in any role, in any way. Being a coach is just my way of "being."

You're reading this book to learn how to be a coach with everyone that you experience. Recognize the greatness in everyone that you meet and in all the changes they're making, big or small. Notice when they might need some more energy, some more help, so that they can move through change in a different way. And be there to be their support and to offer them guidance and encouragement and skills and strategies, and share your life experience with them.

As I'm listening to other people and really wanting for other people to enjoy their life experience and to move through change faster, I use a lot of techniques. The most important technique that I'll introduce you to is the technique of helping people decipher fact from emotion. Let's face it, we've all gone through change that we've been emotional about, and it causes more difficulties and sometimes even slows the pace, brings up a lot of anger, resistance, etc. So as you continue your journey through this book, I want you to remember that as a coach to those that you come in contact with, you want to help each person move through the journey with greater ease and with more joy and delight. You want to do the same for yourself. You'll notice that every single day you get charged about something and so do those you come in contact with. We don't change when we're stuck in a lot of emotion. I carried around an extra 68 pounds on my very short body for many years, being very stuck in the emotion of being angry about being overweight. Why me? This isn't fair! When I was able to release a lot of the emotion and just really look at the truth, the facts, it was a lot easier to choose to change, and I was able to change quickly, because I not only changed by losing weight, I changed by letting go of a lot of the emotion.

As you are preparing for your coaching journey, recognize that this too will change you. No one goes through coach training, be it through a coach training program, through a book about coaching, through working with a coach, or through having a relationship with a friend or family member who has already read this book and been coaching you, without being changed. Look forward to the changes that you will make, not only in yourself, but in others as you help them evolve, grow, enjoy their experience, see their greatness on a bigger scale, meet their goals, exceed their goals, and create an extraordinary life for themselves.

10

Is the Business of Coaching for You?

As you've learned more tools about living your life as a coach and helping other people on this planet enjoy their lives more because of your coaching tools, you may have wondered what it would be like to actually work in the profession of coaching. Certainly, that is an option you may choose, to get some professional training to become a coach and to work part-time, full-time or even develop or create a hobby around coaching. I may be a bit prejudiced, but I strongly believe that anyone who goes through coach training becomes not only a more evolved and better human being, but has a much more wonderfully rewarding life and can share new gifts and new experiences with others. So, I believe whether or not you decide ultimately to use coaching as a way to make your living, you will be a better parent, a better spouse, a better friend, a better partner, a better person, and be more effective in your current relationships, profession, or life, by having formal coach training. If you're wondering, "Is coach training for me?" and "Is the coaching business for me?", I'd like to answer some of those questions here.

If you're looking to have a life that is really very joyful and a life where you feel very much in the moment, in the flow, where there is good energy and where you believe that you create how you choose to experience each and every day and each and every moment, then the coaching profession will open up a realm of possibilities for you. How do you know if having this kind of a life is for you, and if you want to live this kind of a life every day, and be a role model for other people to help them to really live a life that is very simple, uncluttered, and very joyful?

When people approach me about whether or not they should become a coach, or they say it may be their next career but they're not sure, I typically ask them to really think about how they see the world and how they could help others see the world. I see the world as many coaches do, as a wonderfully rewarding, joyful place, one that offers me great experiences, great resources, great time, great energy, and one that is fairly simple to understand. Because I see it that way, I can help clients see it that way and gain greater appreciation, understanding, and joy from their experiences. So the first thing I would take a look at is whether I want to go through coach training and consider becoming a coach, and my answer would be, "Yes, if you would like to have a life that is less complicated and if you would like to have the ability to help other people create a life that's less complicated, one where they have more space, time, freedom, energy, fun, joy, and of course, more play." What would you get out of your coach training that would be most important in the way you live your life, or how others live their life? What I find is that most people who go through coach training, whether they become full-time coaches, part-time coaches, or even choose never to work in the coaching profession, they typically have a simpler way of being. They believe that the present is perfect, that their life is fine just the way it is. They are accepting of the way they are on this planet and the way that other people are, and they behave in a way that supports themselves and other people in achieving each person's unique goals and abilities.

As coaches, we talk a lot about having lives that are balanced and about helping other people get balance in their lives. What

I mean by balance is a feeling that you're resonating at the right vibratory level for who you are and for all the things that are in your life experience. So, perhaps you have the areas of work, community, spirituality, friends, love, relationships, health, wellness, etc., and each of these areas are perfectly balanced for you and is how you choose to experience your life. That doesn't mean that if there are four items on your pie chart of life, that you're spending 25% of your time in each one. It means that you are devoting the time and energy in the area that you choose, and therefore, you are creating a very balanced experience for yourself. If you get excited about creating that for yourself and would love to create that for other people, then coaching may very well be for you. One of the other benefits of coaching is that as coaches, we don't do a lot of struggling. In fact, I talk a lot about the fact that my life is very effortless and that things just come and they flow, I put out to the Universe what I want, I really feel very relaxed, I don't feel a lot of stress, and I spend my time really feeling joyful. This feeling comes from using coaching tools everyday in creating my own life so that I can be the model and really walk my talk. Being a coach is a little bit different than being an accountant or a physician or a sales professional. As a coach, I am expected to walk my talk, each and every day, to do the things that I request of my clients, to be the things that I request my clients be, and to do all of the things that would allow me to live a life of integrity with myself. When I've done that work on myself, and coach training certainly provides us the opportunity to do that work and grow, then I'm ready to help other people in either creating their goals, feeling more balanced, feeling more energy, having more happiness, progressing, overcoming their critical gaps, or learning to be playful again. If you are weighing the decision about coach training, I would also ask you if you have always felt like you were a coach at heart. I would ask if you listen to people and if they really connect with you, and if people like to come to you and speak with you, and if you have always felt most joyful when you are in the experience of seeing other people achieve their own greatness. There is no way that you can be a coach unless in your bones, in your gut, in your soul, you believe that part of the reason you're here on this planet is to serve the world in some fashion and to contribute to the world in some fashion, and for you that means helping other people in their life time experiences.

I was a Speech-Language Pathologist prior to moving into the profession of coaching. While I enjoyed being a Speech-Language Pathologist and later went on to be a corporate executive within the world of healthcare, I noticed that what was most important to me were the times when I was with employees or with my patients training them, educating them, motivating them, developing them, helping them grow, and then I finally recognized what I was doing. One day I exclaimed, "Oh boy, I've been *coaching* them." For me, the shift from Speech Pathology to coaching was natural. As a coach, I don't fix people; everyone is perfect just as they are. No one needs my help, no one needs my fixing, there is no therapy, and I am here to see how the wonderful, successful people who are my clients can achieve even more greatness. As you're deciding whether or not to be a coach, look at your own values; what is your experience about on this planet and how do you see yourself making your own contributions? If it feels completely natural to you to spend time talking with other people, being with other people, and being a role model for other people, and if you really want other people to be successful, and you care deeply about other people's experiences, then you have the stuff that great coaches are made of. I'd also think about how your experience was in reading this book. Did you actually do the exercises? Were you out there tuning in? Were you bringing play to other people? Were you speaking your truth? Were you growing other people? Were you non-judgmental? Were you listening for greatness? Were you celebrating the success of others? It's important to know whether or not, inside of you, you have the desire, the want, to really give back in some way, shape, or form to others through the coaching experience. I believe that many of you who have picked up this book, have picked it up because you're already attracted to the field of coaching and you might not even realize it. Maybe you thought of hiring a coach. Maybe you already have one. Maybe you've been coaching. Maybe you thought about coaching. Maybe you heard about it, or read about it, or something has already resonated with you about the word coaching and the field of coaching. So now you say to me, *coach training, not coach training, make a living out of coaching, not make a living out of coaching.* Please answer that question for me. And I say back to you, "You already know. If you quiet all the voices telling you what you should do and what other people tell you to do. If you go really deep inside, into your own gut, out of your head, and ask yourself, "Would I like to? Would I choose to? Would I want to experience coach training? Would that take me to another level? Would I like to evolve; am I ready?" You'll have your answer. Whether you choose to become a professional coach or not, choose to be more coach-like in your life. You already know how.

Get in touch with whether or not the things in this book have resonated for you in some way. It doesn't mean they all resonated; it means that some hit you and you related to them and got excited about them. It means that you've already had some sense that coaching is right for you.

What if you have fears? Well, fears are absolutely normal. Pretend you're coaching someone; what if they said, "Gee, I might want to start coach training and I might want to become a coach." How would you help them achieve their greatness? What do you see as their critical gap? How can you move them forward? What request would you need to make of them? Or what challenge would you need to offer them? You already know your own truth. Just be authentic. Who are you really inside? Listen to your gut, listen to your heart, and you will be able to make your choice because you already have the answer for yourself.

I will give you one final offering about my experience of becoming a coach and going through coach training, which was the single most powerful decision I have ever made in my lifetime. The gift of coaching and the experience of coach training have brought to me a peaceful, joyful, most wonderful life. I do what I love every single day. I wake up and work with clients, and people, and opportunities that I would want to do regardless of whether anyone ever paid me, because it's part of who I am and why I believe I was put here on our earth. I only know that for myself, something was calling me to coaching. I didn't tune out all the "*shoulds*." I didn't tune out everybody else's voices. I didn't tune out everybody else's wants and desires for me for a period of two years. I wish that I had had the strength, and the courage, and a book like this one to help me get more in touch with who I was and to begin to use coaching tools everyday, because I know that during those two years, I would have chosen to live more as a coach, to be more as a coach, and to get involved in coaching immediately. That's my story. What's yours?

11

Am I Ready for
My Own Coach?

We have almost completed our coaching journey. You've learned a lot along this journey about being coach-like, about coaching others, about improving your own life and even about the field of coaching. I now want to offer you an opportunity to try on coaching, to think about whether it might be right for you to have a coach, to hire a coach, to work with a coach and to really experience being coached through this program in a way that supports the extraordinary life you've chosen to live.

Why do people hire coaches? I think you already have many of these answers. We hire a coach because we want someone who will be non-judgmental, who will truly create a wonderful listening space for us to be ourselves, to find ourselves, and to let us tune out all the "shoulds" that we've come to experience. We hire a coach because we want someone who's going to listen to us and tune in, in a way that we've never been heard before, that's going to allow us to feel more connected to our own energy, our own soul, our own unique being. If you had come to me and asked me to coach you, I would talk with you first to see whether or not coaching is right for you. And what I would be assessing is how ready you are to really make discoveries and make changes. Coaching takes some work on your part. The coach isn't the one who does the work. It's you. You as the client are responsible for making a commitment to the coaching relationship. The coach is there to be your success partner on the journey to help you through the critical gap, to help you see the big, big vision that you haven't seen yet, to help you get from point "A" to point "B" faster than you ever have in your whole life, to help you create more of an extraordinary life than you ever thought possible. The coach will be there to be honest and truthful with you and to help you discover who you are and many strategies and solutions that will allow you to achieve your goals and beyond.

As coaches, we care deeply about our clients and their welfare, and we support them in accomplishing new goals and new behaviors, we acknowledge them and honor them, and recognize their fears, and at the same time, we're there with them, standing in their shoes, and trusting in who they are.

Hire a coach if you're ready to tap into your own inner self, ready to take on new perspectives, and ready to achieve what they said couldn't be done - like that bumblebee who they said should not be able to fly. Hire a coach when you want someone who is going to actively and deeply listen to you and really understand your concerns and your beliefs and your values. I hire a coach because I want someone who's going to ask me powerful questions, who's not going to judge my answer, and who is not in any way, shape, or form, attached to the outcome. My husband, whom I love deeply and who loves me back, is attached to the outcome. We share in a relationship and are deeply connected, so while we're deeply connected it's very difficult to not be attached to the things he wants for me or believes are best for me. That's out of love. I speak with my coaches because they don't care what my goals are or what the outcome is. They simply stand for me and who I am and care about me, Terri, the being inside, as a person. This creates for me greater clarity, greater possibility, and an ability to make decisions that come from inside myself, versus what the world may tell me I should do or what I'm expected to do. Hire a coach because you want to be more aware of yourself and want to learn about your behaviors and your feelings, and because you want to come up with actions that are going to propel you and prepare you for the future and allow you to change in great ways, to exceed your expectations. Hire a coach because you want someone who's going to help you with planning and with goal setting and going to help you tap into different ways of learning and different processes.

Sometimes, people say, "Well maybe I'll hire a therapist or maybe I'll hire a mentor, or maybe I'll hire a consultant. Maybe I won't hire a coach." You'll know if you want to hire a coach if you truly believe that you have your own answers, just as we as coaches already know. You have your own answers about yourself and who you are, and a coach will really help you focus on your future and get in touch with who you are and where you are going. A coach will help you have a stronger way of being and a better human experience. A coach won't give you the answers, but will be your partner in helping you find your own answers and stay with you to implement those answers.

If you want someone to give you all the answers and tell you how to do it, then you're probably looking more for a consultant. If you're looking for someone who's going to help you deal with past issues and a lot of emotional baggage and emotional healing then you're probably looking for a therapist.

Still not sure? Still thinking about hiring a coach? This won't be new to you. I believe you already have the answer for yourself. Has something during your time reading this book made you think, "Gee, I'd like to have a coach." Or "Would it be neat to work with a coach?" Or "I might like to work with a coach." Or "I wonder what the experience would be?" You already have the answer; it's in your gut. You already know. Now take this *knowing* and ask yourself the question, "Do I want to experience coaching?" Get into your gut, get out of your head, stop with the "*shoulds.*" Don't even ask yet what it costs or how you find a coach, just know your own answer.

If coaching resonates for you, if it's right for you, if you're ready to have an experience and at least try on coaching, there are a few resources that will really be helpful to you. First, go visit www.ComprehensiveCoachingU.com and find out more about the many coaches who have been trained by Comprehensive Coaching U, and who love to work with new coaching clients. You can also meet some of the coaches that work with me each and every day by going to www. comprehensivecoachinggroup.com, and there you will see the profiles of the coaches that collaborate with me.

Are you ready to hire your own coach? You know the answer! Many of the coaches at ComprehensiveCoachingU.com will even offer you a free 30 minute complimentary session just to try on coaching, to decide if coaching is right for you, and if the chemistry between you and the coach is right.

How do you know which coach is right for you? It's simply a matter of chemistry. You don't need a coach with special experience, or who knows your exact business, or who has had the same life experiences as you. You need a coach with whom you feel that you can co-create a relationship where you feel comfortable in the space, where you feel connected, where you feel deeply listened to, a coach with whom you'd say, "Gee, I'd love to coach with you." When I hire my own coaches, I typically have two or maybe three complimentary sessions with a couple of different coaches, to try them on and decide which coach matches me best, matches my personality, and matches my chemistry, and decide what it is I'm coming to coaching for. For example, there are diverse kinds of coaches that work with me at Comprehensive Coaching Group. When someone comes to me and says, "Terri, which coach should I hire at Comprehensive Coaching Group?" I tell them to go to the Website, read each person's bio and think about which person just kind of grabs you, or sometimes it's even their photo that grabs you. Then request a complimentary session with two or maybe three of those coaches. Get an idea of what it would be like to work with them in partnership and then hire *your* coach.

What I haven't told you about coaching is that most coaches coach by telephone. I know that probably sounds unique and unusual first time around, sure did to me when I heard that. But coaching really works by telephone. Because we're so connected and we listen so deeply and because we're so tuned into the words and what's underneath the words, the coaching conversation through the telephone is a perfect medium. That's not to say all coaches work by phone, some work in person, many work with groups or teams and some work like I do, where they do most of their coaching by telephone. Some work with organizations in person and then they also do some workshops as well. I wanted to let you know that most coaching is done by phone so that it won't be a shock to you when you begin to contact coaches. It works by telephone, it works, it works! Again, coaching works because you make the commitment to do the work in between the coaching sessions. While most of my clients meet with me by phone three times a month, between our telephone meetings they are doing the work, taking the action, meeting the goals, overcoming obstacles, leaping through their critical gap, listening differently, experiencing life differently, and they are asking themselves different questions. My clients are committed to doing the work and to gaining the light bulb insights that go off after our sessions. So remember, when you're interviewing coaches and when you're pricing out what coaches charge, it's really not about the telephone time, it's really about the entire experience. Coaching is about a process. A process of developing, and growing, and new experiences, and new joys, and a new way of being. It's part of a journey. I invite you to explore this wonderful world of coaching to be a coach, to hire a coach, to get some training as a coach, and to pick this book up again as a resource, as a guide. And as your coach, I encourage you, I honor you, I celebrate you, as you begin your journey in being a role model and beginning to coach everyone that you have experiences with to create a better way of being for yourself and for others. Wishing you a lifetime of creating extraordinary experiences.

Afterword

CREATE MOMENTUM

Okay, it is now time for you to create action now. As your coach, I must ask you to identify the value you received from this book and how you will commit to use your new skills.

I also ask you to know your next action steps. Is it to be a professional coach? Hire a coach? Find out more about coaching? Practice the playwork? Take action today and move yourself, your career, and life to extraordinary new heights.

The journey continues. You are already on the path. I am here to support you.

Coach Terri

How To Contact the Author

Terri Levine, PCC, MS, CCC-SLP, is the founder of Comprehensive Coaching U, Inc., The Professional's Coach Training Program. Comprehensive Coaching U is an internationally recognized program that provides telephone training to individuals and organizations that want to learn coaching skills.

Terri coaches individuals and businesses that want to gain greater personal or business success. She specializes in using Comprehensive Coaching principles to create extraordinary growth for her clients' lives and businesses.

She provides workshops and keynotes around the world and is passionate about sharing coaching tools with audiences at conventions and conferences.

Terri is the author of *Work Yourself Happy* as well as 3 weekly e-mail newsletters with thousands of subscribers worldwide.

She is a nationally recognized authority on creating greater business and personal success and appears regularly in the media for her expertise.

Terri lives in Pennsylvania with her husband, Mark, her dad, Walter, and her dog, Sheba. When she isn't coaching, training, speaking, or writing, she loves to race Formula Dodge cars.

If you are interested in becoming a coach, hiring a coach, or having Terri address your organization, call toll-free 1-877-401-6165 or email info@ComprehensiveCoachingU.com.